STILL MORE ADVANCE NOISE FOR QUIET

ARVIND UPADHYAY

Montgomery, Alabama. December 1, 1955. Early evening. A public bus pulls to a stop and a sensibly dressed woman in her forties gets on. She carries herself erectly, despite having spent the day bent over an ironing board in a dingy basement tailor shop at the Montgomery Fair department store. Her feet are swollen, her shoulders ache. She sits in the first row of the Colored section and watches quietly as the bus fills with riders. Until the driver orders her to give her seat to a white passenger. The woman utters a single word that ignites one of the most important civil rights protests of the twentieth century, one word that helps America find its better self. The word is "No." The driver threatens to have her arrested. "You may do that," says Rosa Parks. A police officer arrives. He asks Parks why she won't move. "Why do you all push us around?" she answers simply. "I don't know," he says. "But the law is the law, and you're under arrest." On the afternoon of her trial and conviction for disorderly conduct, the Montgomery Improvement Association holds a rally for Parks at the Holt Street Baptist Church, in the poorest section of town. Five thousand gather to support Parks's lonely act of courage. They 24/929 squeeze inside the church until its pews can hold no more. The rest wait patiently outside, listening through loudspeakers. The Reverend Martin Luther King Jr. addresses the crowd. "There comes a time that people get tired of being trampled over by the iron feet of oppression," he tells them. "There comes a time when people get tired of being pushed out of the glittering sunlight of life's July and left standing amidst the piercing chill of an Alpine November." He praises Parks's bravery and hugs her. She stands silently, her mere presence enough to galvanize the crowd. The association launches a city-wide bus boycott that lasts 381 days. The people trudge miles to work. They carpool with strangers. They change the course of American history. 25/929 I had always imagined Rosa Parks as a stately woman with a bold temperament, someone who could easily stand up to a busload of glowering passengers. But when she died in 2005 at the age of ninety-two, the flood of obituaries recalled her as soft-spoken, sweet, and small in stature. They said she was "timid and shy" but had "the courage of a lion." They were full of phrases like "radical humility" and "quiet fortitude." What does it mean to be quiet and have fortitude? these descriptions asked implicitly. How could you be shy and courageous? Parks herself seemed aware of this paradox, calling her autobiography Quiet Strength—a title that challenges us to question our assumptions. Why shouldn't quiet be strong? And what else can quiet do that we don't give it credit for? 26/929 Our lives are shaped as profoundly by personality as by gender or race. And the single most important aspect of personality—the "north and south of temperament," as one scientist puts it—is where we fall on the introvert-extrovert spectrum. Our place on this continuum influences our choice of friends and mates, and how we make conversation, resolve differences, and show love. It affects the careers we choose and whether or not we succeed at them. It governs how likely we are to exercise, commit adultery, function well without sleep, learn from our mistakes, place big bets in the stock market, delay gratification, be a good leader, and ask "what if."* It's reflected in our brain pathways, neurotransmitters, and 27/929 remote corners of our nervous systems. Today introversion and extroversion are two of the most exhaustively researched subjects in personality psychology, arousing the curiosity of hundreds of scientists. These researchers have made exciting discoveries aided by the latest technology, but they're part of a long and storied tradition. Poets and philosophers have been thinking about introverts and extroverts since the dawn of recorded time. Both personality types appear in the Bible and in the writings of Greek and Roman physicians, and some evolutionary psychologists say that the history of these types reaches back even farther than that: the animal kingdom also boasts "introverts" and "extroverts," as we'll see, from fruit flies to pumpkinseed fish to rhesus monkeys. As with other complementary 28/929 pairings—masculinity and femininity, East and West, liberal and conservative—humanity would be unrecognizable, and vastly diminished, without both personality styles. Take the partnership of Rosa Parks and Martin Luther King Jr.: a formidable orator refusing to give up his seat on a segregated bus wouldn't have had the same effect as a modest woman who'd clearly prefer to keep silent but for the exigencies of the situation. And Parks didn't have the stuff to thrill a crowd if she'd tried to stand up and announce that she had a dream. But with King's help, she didn't have to. Yet today we make room for a remarkably narrow range of personality styles. We're told that to be great is to be bold, to be happy is to be sociable. We see ourselves as a nation of extroverts—which means that we've lost 29/929 sight of who we really are. Depending on which study you consult, one third to one half of Americans are introverts—in other words, one out of every two or three people you know. (Given that the United States is among the most extroverted of nations, the number must be at least as high in other parts of the world.) If you're not an introvert yourself, you are surely raising, managing, married to, or coupled with one. If these statistics surprise you, that's probably because so many people pretend to be extroverts. Closet introverts pass undetected on playgrounds, in high school locker rooms, and in the corridors of corporate America. Some fool even themselves, until some life event—a layoff, an empty nest, an inheritance that frees them to spend time as they like—jolts them into taking 30/929 stock of their true natures. You have only to raise the subject of this book with your friends and acquaintances to find that the most unlikely people consider themselves introverts. It makes sense that so many introverts hide even from themselves. We live with a value system that I call the Extrovert Ideal—the omnipresent belief that the ideal self is gregarious, alpha, and comfortable in the spotlight. The archetypal extrovert prefers action to contemplation, risk-taking to heed-taking, certainty to doubt. He favors quick decisions, even at the risk of being wrong. She works well in teams and socializes in groups. We like to think that we value individuality, but all too often we admire one type of individual—the kind who's comfortable "putting himself out there." Sure, we allow technologically gifted loners who launch 31/929 companies in garages to have any personality they please, but they are the exceptions, not the rule, and our tolerance extends mainly to those who get fabulously wealthy or hold the promise of doing so. Introversion—along with its cousins sensitivity, seriousness, and shyness—is now a second-class personality trait, somewhere between a disappointment and a pathology. Introverts living under the Extrovert Ideal are like women in a man's world, discounted because of a trait that goes to the core of who they are. Extroversion is an enormously appealing personality style, but we've turned it into an oppressive standard to which most of us feel we must conform. The Extrovert Ideal has been documented in many studies, though this research has never been grouped under a single name. Talkative people, for 32/929 example, are rated as smarter, betterlooking, more interesting, and more desirable as friends. Velocity of speech counts as well as volume: we rank fast talkers as more competent and likable than slow ones. The same dynamics apply in groups, where research shows that the voluble are considered smarter than the reticent—even though there's zero correlation between the gift of gab and good ideas. Even the word introvert is stigmatized—one informal study, by psychologist Laurie Helgoe, found that introverts described their own physical appearance in vivid language ("greenblue eyes," "exotic," "high cheekbones"), but when asked to describe generic introverts they drew a bland and distasteful picture ("ungainly," "neutral colors," "skin problems"). 33/929 But we make a grave mistake to embrace the Extrovert Ideal so unthinkingly. Some of our greatest ideas, art, and inventions—from the theory of evolution to van Gogh's sunflowers to the personal computer—came from quiet and cerebral people who knew how to tune in to their inner worlds and the treasures to be found there. Without introverts, the world would be devoid of: the theory of gravity the theory of relativity W. B. Yeats's "The Second Coming" Chopin's nocturnes Proust's In Search of Lost Time Peter Pan Orwell's Nineteen Eighty-Four and Animal Farm 34/929 The Cat in the Hat Charlie Brown Schindler's List, E.T., and Close Encounters of the Third Kind Google Harry Potter* As the science journalist Winifred Gallagher writes: "The glory of the disposition that stops to consider stimuli rather than rushing to engage with them is its long association with intellectual and artistic achievement. Neither E=mc2 nor Paradise Lost was dashed off by a party animal." Even in less obviously introverted occupations, like finance, politics, and activism, some of the greatest leaps forward were made by introverts. In this book we'll see how figures like Eleanor Roosevelt, Al Gore, Warren Buffett, Gandhi—and 35/929 Rosa Parks—achieved what they did not in spite of but because of their introversion. Yet, as Quiet will explore, many of the most important institutions of contemporary life are designed for those who enjoy group projects and high levels of stimulation. As children, our classroom desks are increasingly arranged in pods, the better to foster group learning, and research suggests that the vast majority of teachers believe that the ideal student is an extrovert. We watch TV shows whose protagonists are not the "children next door," like the Cindy Bradys and Beaver Cleavers of yesteryear, but rock stars and webcast hostesses with outsized personalities, like Hannah Montana and Carly Shay of iCarly. Even Sid the Science Kid, a PBS-sponsored role model for the preschool set, kicks 36/929 off each school day by performing dance moves with his pals. ("Check out my moves! I'm a rock star!") As adults, many of us work for organizations that insist we work in teams, in offices without walls, for supervisors who value "people skills" above all. To advance our careers, we're expected to promote ourselves unabashedly. The scientists whose research gets funded often have confident, perhaps overconfident, personalities. The artists whose work adorns the walls of contemporary museums strike impressive poses at gallery openings. The authors whose books get published—once accepted as a reclusive breed—are now vetted by publicists to make sure they're talk-show ready. (You wouldn't be reading this book if I hadn't convinced my publisher that I was enough of a pseudo-extrovert to promote it.) 37/929

If you're an introvert, you also know that the bias against quiet can cause deep psychic pain. As a child you might have overheard your parents apologize for your shyness. ("Why can't you be more like the Kennedy boys?" the Camelot-besotted parents of one man I interviewed repeatedly asked him.) Or at school you might have been prodded to come "out of your shell"—that noxious expression which fails to appreciate that some animals naturally carry shelter everywhere they go, and that some humans are just the same. "All the comments from childhood still ring in my ears, that I was lazy, stupid, slow, boring," writes a member of an email list called Introvert Retreat. "By the time I was old enough to figure out that I was simply introverted, it was a part of my being, the assumption that there is something inherently wrong 38/929 with me. I wish I could find that little vestige of doubt and remove it." Now that you're an adult, you might still feel a pang of guilt when you decline a dinner invitation in favor of a good book. Or maybe you like to eat alone in restaurants and could do without the pitying looks from fellow diners. Or you're told that you're "in your head too much," a phrase that's often deployed against the quiet and cerebral. Of course, there's another word for such people: thinkers. I have seen firsthand how difficult it is for introverts to take stock of their own talents, and how powerful it is when finally they do. For more than ten years I 39/929 trained people of all stripes—corporate lawyers and college students, hedgefund managers and married couples—in negotiation skills. Of course, we covered the basics: how to prepare for a negotiation, when to make the first offer, and what to do when the other person says "take it or leave it." But I also helped clients figure out their natural personalities and how to make the most of them. My very first client was a young woman named Laura. She was a Wall Street lawyer, but a quiet and daydreamy one who dreaded the spotlight and disliked aggression. She had managed somehow to make it through the crucible of Harvard Law School—a place where classes are conducted in huge, gladiatorial amphitheaters, and where she once got so nervous that she threw up on the way to class. Now that 40/929 she was in the real world, she wasn't sure she could represent her clients as forcefully as they expected. For the first three years on the job, Laura was so junior that she never had to test this premise. But one day the senior lawyer she'd been working with went on vacation, leaving her in charge of an important negotiation. The client was a South American manufacturing company that was about to default on a bank loan and hoped to renegotiate its terms; a syndicate of bankers that owned the endangered loan sat on the other side of the negotiating table. Laura would have preferred to hide under said table, but she was accustomed to fighting such impulses. Gamely but nervously, she took her spot in the lead chair, flanked by her clients: general counsel on one side and senior financial officer on the other. 41/929 These happened to be Laura's favorite clients: gracious and soft-spoken, very different from the master-of-the-universe types her firm usually represented. In the past, Laura had taken the general counsel to a Yankees game and the financial officer shopping for a handbag for her sister. But now these cozy outings—just the kind of socializing Laura enjoyed—seemed a world away. Across the table sat nine disgruntled investment bankers in tailored suits and expensive shoes, accompanied by their lawyer, a square-jawed woman with a hearty manner. Clearly not the self-doubting type, this woman launched into an impressive speech on how Laura's clients would be lucky simply to accept the bankers' terms. It was, she said, a very magnanimous offer. 42/929 Everyone waited for Laura to reply, but she couldn't think of anything to say. So she just sat there. Blinking. All eyes on her. Her clients shifting uneasily in their seats. Her thoughts running in a familiar loop: I'm too quiet for this kind of thing, too unassuming, too cerebral. She imagined the person who would be better equipped to save the day: someone bold, smooth, ready to pound the table. In middle school this person, unlike Laura, would have been called "outgoing," the highest accolade her seventh-grade classmates knew, higher even than "pretty," for a girl, or "athletic," for a guy. Laura promised herself that she only had to make it through the day. Tomorrow she would go look for another career. Then she remembered what I'd told her again and again: she was an introvert, and as such she had unique 43/929 powers in negotiation—perhaps less obvious but no less formidable. She'd probably prepared more than everyone else. She had a quiet but firm speaking style. She rarely spoke without thinking. Being mild-mannered, she could take strong, even aggressive, positions while coming across as perfectly reasonable. And she tended to ask questions—lots of them—and actually listen to the answers, which, no matter what your personality, is crucial to strong negotiation. So Laura finally started doing what came naturally. "Let's go back a step. What are your numbers based on?" she asked. "What if we structured the loan this way, do you think it might work?" "That way?" "Some other way?" 44/929 At first her questions were tentative. She picked up steam as she went along, posing them more forcefully and making it clear that she'd done her homework and wouldn't concede the facts. But she also stayed true to her own style, never raising her voice or losing her decorum. Every time the bankers made an assertion that seemed unbudgeable, Laura tried to be constructive. "Are you saying that's the only way to go? What if we took a different approach?" Eventually her simple queries shifted the mood in the room, just as the negotiation textbooks say they will. The bankers stopped speechifying and dominance-posing, activities for which Laura felt hopelessly ill-equipped, and they started having an actual conversation. 45/929 More discussion. Still no agreement. One of the bankers revved up again, throwing his papers down and storming out of the room. Laura ignored this display, mostly because she didn't know what else to do. Later on someone told her that at that pivotal moment she'd played a good game of something called "negotiation jujitsu"; but she knew that she was just doing what you learn to do naturally as a quiet person in a loudmouth world. Finally the two sides struck a deal. The bankers left the building, Laura's favorite clients headed for the airport, and Laura went home, curled up with a book, and tried to forget the day's tensions. But the next morning, the lead lawyer for the bankers—the vigorous woman with the strong jaw—called to offer her a job. "I've never seen anyone 46/929 so nice and so tough at the same time," she said.

And the day after that, the lead banker called Laura, asking if her law firm would represent his company in the future. "We need someone who can help us put deals together without letting ego get in the way," he said. By sticking to her own gentle way of doing things, Laura had reeled in new business for her firm and a job offer for herself. Raising her voice and pounding the table was unnecessary. Today Laura understands that her introversion is an essential part of who she is, and she embraces her reflective nature. The loop inside her head that accused her of being too quiet and unassuming plays much less often. Laura knows that she can hold her own when she needs to. 47/ 929 What exactly do I mean when I say that Laura is an introvert? When I started writing this book, the first thing I wanted to find out was precisely how researchers define introversion and extroversion. I knew that in 1921 the influential psychologist Carl Jung had published a bombshell of a book, Psychological Types, popularizing the terms introvert and extrovert as the central building blocks of personality. Introverts are drawn to the inner world of thought and feeling, said Jung, extroverts to the external life of people and activities. Introverts focus on the meaning they make of the events swirling around them; extroverts plunge into the events themselves. Introverts recharge their batteries by being alone; 48/929 extroverts need to recharge when they don't socialize enough. If you've ever taken a Myers-Briggs personality test, which is based on Jung's thinking and used by the majority of universities and Fortune 100 companies, then you may already be familiar with these ideas. But what do contemporary researchers have to say? I soon discovered that there is no all-purpose definition of introversion or extroversion; these are not unitary categories, like "curlyhaired" or "sixteen-year-old," in which everyone can agree on who qualifies for inclusion. For example, adherents of the Big Five school of personality psychology (which argues that human personality can be boiled down to five primary traits) define introversion not in terms of a rich inner life but as a lack of qualities such as assertiveness and sociability. There are almost as 49/929 many definitions of introvert and extrovert as there are personality psychologists, who spend a great deal of time arguing over which meaning is most accurate. Some think that Jung's ideas are outdated; others swear that he's the only one who got it right. Still, today's psychologists tend to agree on several important points: for example, that introverts and extroverts differ in the level of outside stimulation that they need to function well. Introverts feel "just right" with less stimulation, as when they sip wine with a close friend, solve a crossword puzzle, or read a book. Extroverts enjoy the extra bang that comes from activities like meeting new people, skiing slippery slopes, and cranking up the stereo. "Other people are very arousing," says the personality psychologist David Winter, explaining why your typical 50/929 introvert would rather spend her vacation reading on the beach than partying on a cruise ship. "They arouse threat, fear, flight, and love. A hundred people are very stimulating compared to a hundred books or a hundred grains of sand." Many psychologists would also agree that introverts and extroverts work differently. Extroverts tend to tackle assignments quickly. They make fast (sometimes rash) decisions, and are comfortable multitasking and risk-taking. They enjoy "the thrill of the chase" for rewards like money and status. Introverts often work more slowly and deliberately. They like to focus on one task at a time and can have mighty powers of concentration. They're relatively immune to the lures of wealth and fame. 51/929 Our personalities also shape our social styles. Extroverts are the people who will add life to your dinner party and laugh generously at your jokes. They tend to be assertive, dominant, and in great need of company. Extroverts think out loud and on their feet; they prefer talking to listening, rarely find themselves at a loss for words, and occasionally blurt out things they never meant to say. They're comfortable with conflict, but not with solitude. Introverts, in contrast, may have strong social skills and enjoy parties and business meetings, but after a while wish they were home in their pajamas. They prefer to devote their social energies to close friends, colleagues, and family. They listen more than they talk, think before they speak, and often feel as if they express themselves better in writing than in 52/929 conversation. They tend to dislike conflict. Many have a horror of small talk, but enjoy deep discussions. A few things introverts are not: The word introvert is not a synonym for hermit or misanthrope. Introverts can be these things, but most are perfectly friendly. One of the most humane phrases in the English language—"Only connect!"—was written by the distinctly introverted E. M. Forster in a novel exploring the question of how to achieve "human love at its height." Nor are introverts necessarily shy. Shyness is the fear of social disapproval or humiliation, while introversion is a preference for environments that are not overstimulating. Shyness is inherently painful; introversion is not. One reason that people confuse the two concepts is that they sometimes overlap (though psychologists debate to what 53/929 degree). Some psychologists map the two tendencies on vertical and horizontal axes, with the introvert-extrovert spectrum on the horizontal axis, and the anxious-stable spectrum on the vertical. With this model, you end up with four quadrants of personality types: calm extroverts, anxious (or impulsive) extroverts, calm introverts, and anxious introverts. In other words, you can be a shy extrovert, like Barbra Streisand, who has a larger-than-life personality and paralyzing stage fright; or a nonshy introvert, like Bill Gates, who by all accounts keeps to himself but is unfazed by the opinions of others. You can also, of course, be both shy and an introvert: T. S. Eliot was a famously private soul who wrote in "The Waste Land" that he could "show you fear in a handful of dust." Many shy people turn inward, partly as a refuge 54/929 from the socializing that causes them such anxiety. And many introverts are shy, partly as a result of receiving the message that there's something wrong with their preference for reflection, and partly because their physiologies, as we'll see, compel them to withdraw from high-stimulation environments.

But for all their differences, shyness and introversion have in common something profound. The mental state of a shy extrovert sitting quietly in a business meeting may be very different from that of a calm introvert—the shy person is afraid to speak up,

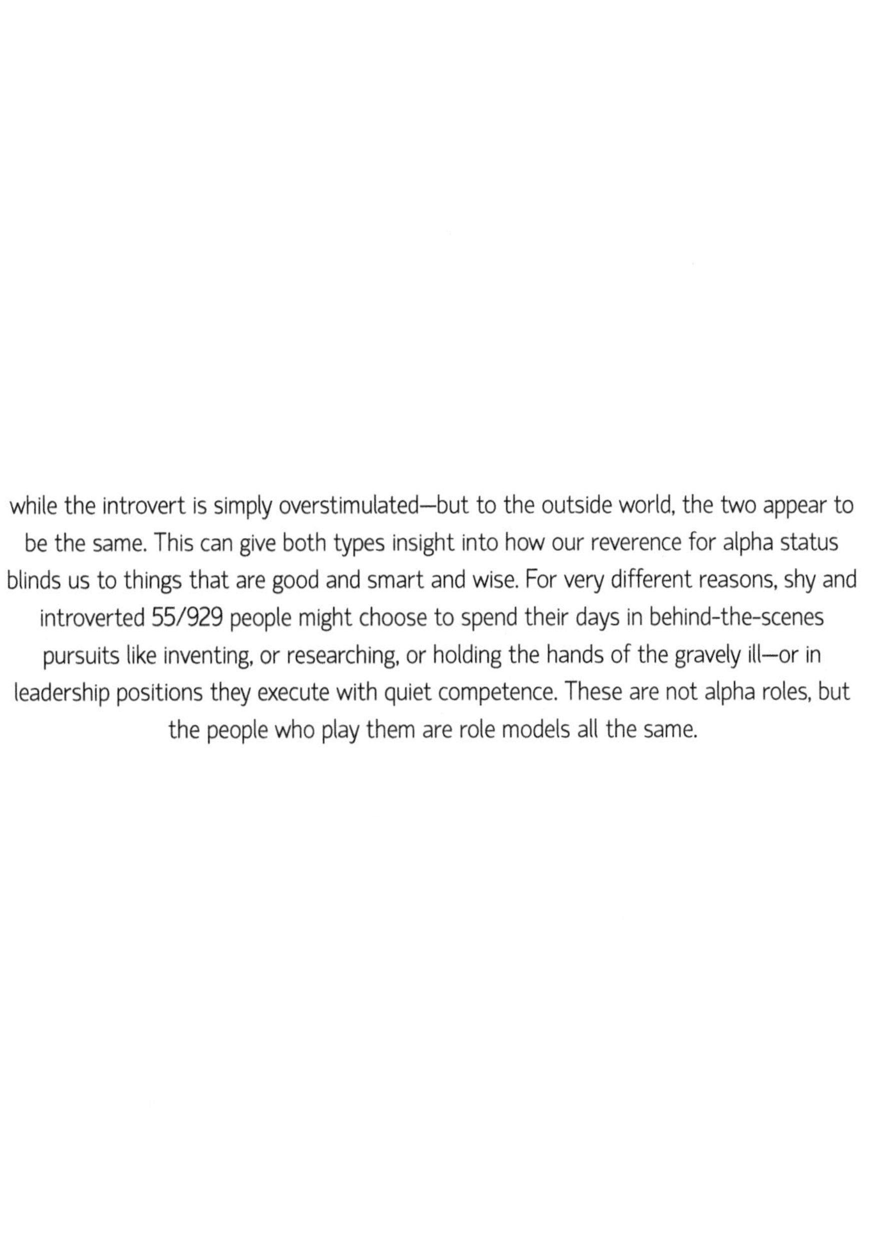

while the introvert is simply overstimulated—but to the outside world, the two appear to be the same. This can give both types insight into how our reverence for alpha status blinds us to things that are good and smart and wise. For very different reasons, shy and introverted 55/929 people might choose to spend their days in behind-the-scenes pursuits like inventing, or researching, or holding the hands of the gravely ill—or in leadership positions they execute with quiet competence. These are not alpha roles, but the people who play them are role models all the same.

Contents

Foreword

If you're still not sure where you fall on the introvert-extrovert spectrum, you can assess yourself here. Answer each question "true" or "false," choosing the answer that applies to you more often than not.* 1. _______ I prefer one-on-one conversations to group activities. 2. _______ I often prefer to express myself in writing. 3. _______ I enjoy solitude. 4. _______ I seem to care less than my peers about wealth, fame, and status. 5. _______ I dislike small talk, but I enjoy talking in depth about topics that matter to me. 6. _______ People tell me that I'm a good listener. 7. _______ I'm not a big risk-taker. 8. _______ I enjoy work that allows me to "dive in" with few interruptions. 9. _______ I like to celebrate birthdays on a small scale, with only one or two close friends or family members. 10. _______ People describe me as "softspoken" or "mellow." 11. _______ I prefer not to show or discuss my work with others until it's finished. 12. _______ I dislike conflict. 13. _______ I do my best work on my own. 14. _______ I tend to think before I speak. 15. _______ I feel drained after being out and about, even if I've enjoyed myself. 16. _______ I often let calls go through to voice mail. 17. _______ If I had to choose, I'd prefer a weekend with absolutely nothing to do to one with too many things scheduled. 18. _______ I don't enjoy multitasking. 19. _______ I can concentrate easily. 20. _______ In classroom situations, I prefer lectures to seminars. The more often you answered "true," the more introverted you probably are. If you found yourself with a roughly equal number of "true" and "false" answers, then you may be an ambivert—yes, there really is such a word. But even if you answered every single question as an introvert or extrovert, that doesn't mean that your behavior is predictable across all circumstances. We can't say that every introvert is a bookworm or every extrovert wears lampshades at parties any more than we can say that every woman is a natural consensus-builder and every man loves contact sports. As Jung felicitously put it, "There is no such thing as a pure extrovert or a pure introvert. Such a man would be in the lunatic asylum." This is partly because we are all gloriously complex individuals, but also because there are so many different kinds of introverts and extroverts. Introversion and extroversion interact with our other personality traits and personal histories, producing wildly different kinds of people. So if you're an artistic American guy whose father wished you'd try out for the football team like

"

your rough-and-tumble brothers, you'll be a very different kind of introvert from, say, a Finnish businesswoman whose parents were lighthouse keepers. (Finland is a famously introverted nation. Finnish joke: How can you tell if a Finn likes you? He's staring at your shoes instead of his own.) Many introverts are also "highly sensitive," which sounds poetic, but is actually a technical term in psychology. If you are a sensitive sort, then you're more apt than the average person to feel pleasantly overwhelmed by Beethoven's "Moonlight Sonata" or a wellturned phrase or an act of extraordinary kindness. You may be quicker than others to feel sickened by violence and ugliness, and you likely have a very strong conscience. When you were a child you were probably called "shy," and to this day feel nervous when you're being evaluated, for example when giving a speech or on a first date. Later we'll examine why this seemingly unrelated collection of attributes tends to belong to the same person and why this person is often introverted. (No one knows exactly how many introverts are highly sensitive, but we know that 70 percent of sensitives are introverts, and 61/ 929 the other 30 percent tend to report needing a lot of "down time.") All of this complexity means that not everything you read in Quiet will apply to you, even if you consider yourself a true-blue introvert. For one thing, we'll spend some time talking about shyness and sensitivity, while you might have neither of these traits. That's OK. Take what applies to you, and use the rest to improve your relationships with others. Having said all this, in Quiet we'll try not to get too hung up on definitions. Strictly defining terms is vital for researchers whose studies depend on pinpointing exactly where introversion stops and other traits, like shyness, start. But in Quiet we'll concern ourselves more with the fruit of that research. Today's psychologists, joined by neuroscientists with their brain-scanning machines, have unearthed illuminating insights that are changing the way we see the world—and ourselves. They are answering questions such as: Why are some people talkative while others measure their words? Why do some people burrow into their work and others organize office birthday parties? Why are some people comfortable wielding authority while others prefer neither to lead nor to be led? Can introverts be leaders? Is our cultural preference for extroversion in the natural order of things, or is it socially determined? From an evolutionary perspective, introversion must have survived as a personality trait for a reason—so what might the reason be? If you're an introvert, should you devote your energies to activities that come naturally, or should you stretch yourself, as Laura did that day at the negotiation table? The answers might surprise you. If there is only one insight you take away from this book, though, I hope it's a newfound sense of entitlement to be yourself. I can vouch personally for the life-transforming effects of this outlook. Remember that first client I told you about, the one I called Laura in order to protect her identity? That was a story about me. I was my own first client.

CHAPTER ONE

How Extroversion Became the Cultural Ideal

The date: 1902. The place: Harmony Church, Missouri, a tiny, dot-on-themap town located on a floodplain a hundred miles from Kansas City. Our young protagonist: a good-natured but insecure high school student named Dale. Skinny, unathletic, and fretful, Dale is the son of a morally upright but perpetually bankrupt pig farmer. He respects his parents but dreads following in their poverty-stricken footsteps. Dale worries about other things, too: thunder and lightning, going to hell, and being tongue-tied at crucial moments. He even fears his wedding day: What if he can't think of anything to say to his future bride? One day a Chautauqua speaker comes to town. The Chautauqua movement, born in 1873 and based in upstate New York, sends gifted speakers across the country to lecture on literature, science, and religion. Rural Americans prize these presenters for the whiff of glamour they bring from the outside world—and their power to 68/929 mesmerize an audience. This particular speaker captivates the young Dale with his own rags-to-riches tale: once he'd been a lowly farm boy with a bleak future, but he developed a charismatic speaking style and took the stage at Chautauqua. Dale hangs on his every word. A few years later, Dale is again impressed by the value of public speaking. His family moves to a farm three miles outside of Warrensburg, Missouri, so he can attend college there without paying room and board. Dale observes that the students who win campus speaking contests are seen as leaders, and he resolves to be one of them. He signs up for every contest and rushes home at night to practice. Again and again he loses; Dale is dogged, but not much of an orator. Eventually, though, his efforts begin to pay off. He transforms 69/929 himself into a speaking champion and campus hero. Other students turn to him for speech lessons; he trains them and they start winning, too. By the time Dale leaves college in 1908, his parents are still poor, but corporate America is booming. Henry Ford is selling Model Ts like griddle cakes, using the slogan "for business and for pleasure." J.C. Penney, Woolworth, and Sears Roebuck have become household names. Electricity lights up the homes of the middle class; indoor plumbing spares them midnight trips to the outhouse. The new economy calls for a new kind of man—a salesman, a social operator, someone with a ready smile, a masterful handshake, and the ability to get along with colleagues while simultaneously outshining them. Dale joins the swelling ranks of salesmen, heading 70/929 out on the road with few possessions but his silver tongue. Dale's last name is Carnegie (Carnagey, actually; he changes the spelling later, likely to evoke Andrew, the great industrialist). After a few grueling years selling beef for Armour and Company, he sets up shop as a public-speaking teacher. Carnegie holds his first class at a YMCA night school on 125th Street in New York City. He asks for the usual two-dollars-per-session salary for night school teachers. The Y's director, doubting that a publicspeaking class will generate much interest, refuses to pay that kind of money. But the class is an overnight sensation, and Carnegie goes on to found the Dale Carnegie Institute, dedicated to helping businessmen root out the very insecurities that had held him back as a 71/929 young man. In 1913 he publishes his first book, Public Speaking and Influencing Men in Business. "In the days when pianos and bathrooms were luxuries," Carnegie writes, "men regarded ability in speaking as a peculiar gift, needed only by the lawyer, clergyman, or statesman. Today we have come to realize that it is the indispensable weapon of those who would forge ahead in the keen competition of business." Carnegie's metamorphosis from farmboy to salesman to public-speaking icon is also the story of the rise of the Extrovert Ideal. Carnegie's journey reflected a cultural evolution that reached a tipping point around the turn of the 72/929 twentieth century, changing forever who we are and whom we admire, how we act at job interviews and what we look for in an employee, how we court our mates and raise our children. America had shifted from what the influential cultural historian Warren Susman called a Culture of Character to a Culture of Personality—and opened up a Pandora's Box of personal anxieties from which we would never quite recover. In the Culture of Character, the ideal self was serious, disciplined, and honorable. What counted was not so much the impression one made in public as how one behaved in private. The word personality didn't exist in English until the eighteenth century, and the idea of "having a good personality" was not widespread until the twentieth. 73/929 But when they embraced the Culture of Personality, Americans started to focus on how others perceived them. They became captivated by people who were bold and entertaining. "The social role demanded of all in the new Culture of Personality was that of a performer," Susman famously wrote. "Every American was to become a performing self." The rise of industrial America was a major force behind this cultural evolution. The nation quickly developed from an agricultural society of little houses on the prairie to an urbanized, "the business of America is business" powerhouse. In the country's early days, most Americans lived like Dale Carnegie's family, on farms or in small towns, interacting with people they'd known since childhood. But when the twentieth century arrived, a perfect storm of big business, urbanization, and 74/929 mass immigration blew the population into the cities. In 1790, only 3 percent of Americans lived in cities; in 1840, only 8 percent did; by 1920, more than a third of the country were urbanites. "We cannot all live in cities," wrote the news editor Horace Greeley in 1867, "yet nearly all seem determined to do so." Americans found themselves working no longer with neighbors but with strangers. "Citizens" morphed into "employees," facing the question of how to make a good impression on people to whom they had no civic or family ties. "The reasons why one man gained a promotion or one woman suffered a social snub," writes the historian Roland Marchand, "had become less explicable on grounds of long-standing favoritism or old family feuds. In the increasingly anonymous business and social 75/929 relationships of the age, one might suspect that anything—including a first impression—had made the crucial difference." Americans responded to these pressures by trying to become salesmen who could sell not only their company's latest gizmo but also themselves. One of the most powerful lenses through which to view the transformation from Character to Personality is the self-help tradition in which Dale Carnegie played such a prominent role. Self-help books have always loomed large in the American psyche. Many of the earliest conduct guides were religious parables, like The Pilgrim's Progress, published in 1678, which warned readers to behave with restraint if they wanted to make it into heaven. The advice manuals of the nineteenth century were less religious but still preached the value of a noble character. They 76/929 featured case studies of historical heroes like Abraham Lincoln, revered not only as a gifted communicator but also as a modest man who did not, as Ralph Waldo Emerson put it, "offend by superiority."

They also celebrated regular people who lived highly moral lives. A popular 1899 manual called Character: The Grandest Thing in the World featured a timid shop girl who gave away her meager earnings to a freezing beggar, then rushed off before anyone could see what she'd done. Her virtue, the reader understood, derived not only from her generosity but also from her wish to remain anonymous. But by 1920, popular self-help guides had changed their focus from inner virtue to outer charm—"to know what to say and how to say it," as one manual put it. "To create a personality is power," advised another. "Try in every 77/929 way to have a ready command of the manners which make people think 'he's a mighty likeable fellow,' " said a third. "That is the beginning of a reputation for personality." Success magazine and The Saturday Evening Post introduced departments instructing readers on the art of conversation. The same author, Orison Swett Marden, who wrote Character: The Grandest Thing in the World in 1899, produced another popular title in 1921. It was called Masterful Personality. Many of these guides were written for businessmen, but women were also urged to work on a mysterious quality called "fascination." Coming of age in the 1920s was such a competitive business compared to what their grandmothers had experienced, warned one beauty guide, that they had to be visibly charismatic: "People who pass us 78/929 on the street can't know that we're clever and charming unless we look it." Such advice—ostensibly meant to improve people's lives—must have made even reasonably confident people uneasy. Susman counted the words that appeared most frequently in the personality-driven advice manuals of the early twentieth century and compared them to the character guides of the nineteenth century. The earlier guides emphasized attributes that anyone could work on improving, described by words like Citizenship Duty Work Golden deeds Honor Reputation Morals 79/929 Manners Integrity But the new guides celebrated qualities that were—no matter how easy Dale Carnegie made it sound—trickier to acquire. Either you embodied these qualities or you didn't: Magnetic Fascinating Stunning Attractive Glowing Dominant Forceful Energetic It was no coincidence that in the 1920s and the 1930s, Americans became obsessed with movie stars. Who 80/929 better than a matinee idol to model personal magnetism? Americans also received advice on selfpresentation—whether they liked it or not—from the advertising industry. While early print ads were straightforward product announcements ("EATON'S HIGHLAND LINEN: THE FRESHEST AND CLEANEST WRITING PAPER"), the new personalitydriven ads cast consumers as performers with stage fright from which only the advertiser's product might rescue them. These ads focused obsessively on the hostile glare of the public spotlight. "ALL AROUND YOU PEOPLE ARE JUDGING YOU SILENTLY," warned a 1922 ad for Woodbury's soap. "CRITICAL EYES ARE 81/929 SIZING YOU UP RIGHT NOW," advised the Williams Shaving Cream company. Madison Avenue spoke directly to the anxieties of male salesmen and middle managers. In one ad for Dr. West's toothbrushes, a prosperous-looking fellow sat behind a desk, his arm cocked confidently behind his hip, asking whether you've "EVER TRIED SELLING YOURSELF TO YOU? A FAVORABLE FIRST IMPRESSION IS THE GREATEST SINGLE FACTOR IN BUSINESS OR SOCIAL SUCCESS." The Williams Shaving Cream ad featured a slickhaired, mustachioed man urging readers to "LET YOUR FACE REFLECT CONFIDENCE, NOT WORRY! IT'S THE 'LOOK' OF YOU BY WHICH YOU ARE JUDGED MOST OFTEN." Other ads reminded women that their success in the dating game depended not only on looks but also on personality. In 1921 a Woodbury's soap ad 82/929 showed a crestfallen young woman, home alone after a disappointing evening out. She had "longed to be successful, gay, triumphant," the text sympathized. But without the help of the right soap, the woman was a social failure. Ten years later, Lux laundry detergent ran a print ad featuring a plaintive letter written to Dorothy Dix, the Dear Abby of her day. "Dear Miss Dix," read the letter, "How can I make myself more popular? I am fairly pretty and not a dumbbell, but I am so timid and self-conscious with people. I'm always sure they're not going to like me.... —Joan G." Miss Dix's answer came back clear and firm. If only Joan would use Lux detergent on her lingerie, curtains, and sofa cushions, she would soon gain a "deep, sure, inner conviction of being charming." 83/929 This portrayal of courtship as a highstakes performance reflected the bold new mores of the Culture of Personality. Under the restrictive (in some cases repressive) social codes of the Culture of Character, both genders displayed some reserve when it came to the mating dance. Women who were too loud or made inappropriate eye contact with strangers were considered brazen. Upper-class women had more license to speak than did their lower-class counterparts, and indeed were judged partly on their talent for witty repartee, but even they were advised to display blushes and downcast eyes. They were warned by conduct manuals that "the coldest reserve" was "more admirable in a woman a man wishe[d] to make his wife than the least approach to undue familiarity." Men could adopt a quiet demeanor that implied self84/929 possession and a power that didn't need to flaunt itself. Though shyness per se was unacceptable, reserve was a mark of good breeding. But with the advent of the Culture of Personality, the value of formality began to crumble, for women and men alike. Instead of paying ceremonial calls on women and making serious declarations of intention, men were now expected to launch verbally sophisticated courtships in which they threw women "a line" of elaborate flirtatiousness. Men who were too quiet around women risked being thought gay; as a popular 1926 sex guide observed, "homosexuals are invariably timid, shy, retiring." Women, too, were expected to walk a fine line between propriety and boldness. If they responded too shyly to romantic overtures, they were sometimes called "frigid." 85/929 The field of psychology also began to grapple with the pressure to project confidence. In the 1920s an influential psychologist named Gordon Allport created a diagnostic test of "AscendanceSubmission" to measure social dominance. "Our current civilization," observed Allport, who was himself shy and reserved, "seems to place a premium upon the aggressive person, the 'gogetter.' " In 1921, Carl Jung noted the newly precarious status of introversion. Jung himself saw introverts as "educators and promoters of culture" who showed the value of "the interior life which is so painfully wanting in our civilization." But he acknowledged that their "reserve and apparently groundless embarrassment naturally arouse all the current prejudices against this type." 86/929 But nowhere was the need to appear self-assured more apparent than in a new concept in psychology called the inferiority complex. The IC, as it became known in the popular press, was developed in the 1920s by a Viennese psychologist named Alfred Adler to describe feelings of inadequacy and their consequences. "Do you feel insecure?" inquired the cover of Adler's bestselling book, Understanding Human Nature. "Are you fainthearted? Are you submissive?" Adler explained that all infants and small children feel inferior, living as they do in a world of adults and older siblings. In the normal process of growing up they learn to direct these feelings into pursuing their goals. But if things go awry as they mature, they might be saddled with the dreaded IC—a grave liability in an increasingly competitive society. 87/929 The idea of wrapping their social anxieties in the neat package of a psychological complex appealed to many Americans. The Inferiority Complex became an all-purpose explanation for problems in many areas of life, ranging from love to parenting to career. In 1924, Collier's ran a story about a woman who was afraid to marry the man she loved for fear that he had an IC and would never amount to anything. Another popular magazine ran an article called "Your Child and That Fashionable Complex," explaining to moms what could cause an IC in kids and how to prevent or cure one. Everyone had an IC, it seemed; to some it was, paradoxically enough, a mark of distinction. Lincoln, Napoleon, Teddy Roosevelt, Edison, and Shakespeare—all had suffered from ICs, according to a 1939 Collier's article. "So," concluded the 88/929 magazine, "if you have a big, husky, ingrowing inferiority complex you're about as lucky as you could hope to be, provided you have the backbone along with it." Despite the hopeful tone of this piece, child guidance experts of the 1920s set about helping children to develop winning personalities. Until then, these professionals had worried mainly about sexually precocious girls and delinquent boys, but now psychologists, social workers, and doctors focused on the everyday child with the "maladjusted personality"—particularly shy children. Shyness could lead to dire outcomes, they warned, from alcoholism to suicide, while an outgoing personality would bring social and financial success. The experts advised parents to socialize their children well and schools to change their emphasis from book89/929 learning to "assisting and guiding the developing personality." Educators took up this mantle enthusiastically. By 1950 the slogan of the Mid-Century White House Conference on Children and Youth was "A healthy personality for every child." Well-meaning parents of the midcentury agreed that quiet was unacceptable and gregariousness ideal for both girls and boys. Some discouraged their children from solitary and serious hobbies, like classical music, that could make them unpopular. They sent their kids to school at increasingly young ages, where the main assignment was learning to socialize. Introverted children were often singled out as problem cases (a situation familiar to anyone with an introverted child today). William Whyte's The Organization Man, a 1956 best-seller, describes how 90/929 parents and teachers conspired to overhaul the personalities of quiet children. "Johnny wasn't doing so well at school," Whyte recalls a mother telling him. "The teacher explained to me that he was doing fine on his lessons but that his social adjustment was not as good as it might be. He would pick just one or two friends to play with, and sometimes he was happy to remain by himself." Parents welcomed such interventions, said Whyte. "Save for a few odd parents, most are grateful that the schools work so hard to offset tendencies to introversion and other suburban abnormalities." Parents caught up in this value system were not unkind, or even obtuse; they were only preparing their kids for the "real world." When these children grew older and applied to college and later for their first jobs, they faced the 91/929 same standards of gregariousness. University admissions officers looked not for the most exceptional candidates, but for the most extroverted. Harvard's provost Paul Buck declared in the late 1940s that Harvard should reject the "sensitive, neurotic" type and the "intellectually over-stimulated" in favor of boys of the "healthy extrovert kind." In 1950, Yale's president, Alfred Whitney Griswold, declared that the ideal Yalie was not a "beetle-browed, highly specialized intellectual, but a wellrounded man." Another dean told Whyte that "in screening applications from secondary schools he felt it was only common sense to take into account not only what the college wanted, but what, four years later, corporations' recruiters would want. 'They like a pretty gregarious, active type,' he said. 'So we find that the best man is 92/929 the one who's had an 80 or 85 average in school and plenty of extracurricular activity. We see little use for the "brilliant" introvert.' " This college dean grasped very well that the model employee of the midcentury—even one whose job rarely involved dealing with the public, like a research scientist in a corporate lab—was not a deep thinker but a hearty extrovert with a salesman's personality. "Customarily, whenever the word brilliant is used," explains Whyte, "it either precedes the word 'but' (e.g., 'We are all for brilliance, but ...') or is coupled with such words as erratic, eccentric, introvert, screwball, etc." "These fellows will be having contact with other people in the organization," said one 1950s executive about the hapless scientists in his employ, "and it helps if they make a good impression." 93/929 The scientist's job was not only to do the research but also to help sell it, and that required a hail-fellow-well-met demeanor. At IBM, a corporation that embodied the ideal of the company man, the sales force gathered each morning to belt out the company anthem, "Ever Onward," and to harmonize on the "Selling IBM" song, set to the tune of "Singin' in the Rain." "Selling IBM," it began, "we're selling IBM. What a glorious feeling, the world is our friend." The ditty built to a stirring close: "We're always in trim, we work with a vim. We're selling, just selling, IBM." Then they went off to pay their sales calls, proving that the admissions people at Harvard and Yale were probably right: only a certain type of fellow could possibly have been interested in kicking off his mornings this way. 94/929 The rest of the organization men would have to manage as best they could. And if the history of pharmaceutical consumption is any indication, many buckled under such pressures. In 1955 a drug company named CarterWallace released the anti-anxiety drug Miltown, reframing anxiety as the natural product of a society that was both dog-eat-dog and relentlessly social. Miltown was marketed to men and immediately became the fastest-selling pharmaceutical in American history, according to the social historian Andrea Tone. By 1956 one of every twenty Americans had tried it; by 1960 a third of all prescriptions from U.S. doctors were for Miltown or a similar drug called Equanil. "ANXIETY AND TENSION ARE THE COMMONPLACE OF THE AGE," read the Equanil ad. The 1960s tranquilizer Serentil followed with an ad campaign 95/929 even more direct in its appeal to improve social performance. "FOR THE ANXIETY THAT COMES FROM NOT FITTING IN," it empathized. Of course, the Extrovert Ideal is not a modern invention. Extroversion is in our DNA—literally, according to some psychologists. The trait has been found to be less prevalent in Asia and Africa than in Europe and America, whose populations descend largely from the migrants of the world. It makes sense, say these researchers, that world travelers were more extroverted than those who stayed home—and that they passed on their traits to their children and their children's children. "As 96/929 personality traits are genetically transmitted," writes the psychologist Kenneth Olson, "each succeeding wave of emigrants to a new continent would give rise over time to a population of more engaged individuals than reside in the emigrants' continent of origin." We can also trace our admiration of extroverts to the Greeks, for whom oratory was an exalted skill, and to the Romans, for whom the worst possible punishment was banishment from the city, with its teeming social life. Similarly, we revere our founding fathers precisely because they were loudmouths on the subject of freedom: Give me liberty or give me death! Even the Christianity of early American religious revivals, dating back to the First Great Awakening of the eighteenth century, depended on the showmanship of ministers who were considered successful if 97/929 they caused crowds of normally reserved people to weep and shout and generally lose their decorum. "Nothing gives me more pain and distress than to see a minister standing almost motionless, coldly plodding on as a mathematician would calculate the distance of the Moon from the Earth," complained a religious newspaper in 1837. As this disdain suggests, early Americans revered action and were suspicious of intellect, associating the life of the mind with the languid, ineffectual European aristocracy they had left behind. The 1828 presidential campaign pitted a former Harvard professor, John Quincy Adams, against Andrew Jackson, a forceful military hero. A Jackson campaign slogan tellingly distinguished the two: "John Quincy Adams who can write / And Andrew Jackson who can fight." 98/929 The victor of that campaign? The fighter beat the writer, as the cultural historian Neal Gabler puts it. (John Quincy Adams, incidentally, is considered by political psychologists to be one of the few introverts in presidential history.) But the rise of the Culture of Personality intensified such biases, and applied them not only to political and religious leaders, but also to regular people. And though soap manufacturers may have profited from the new emphasis on charm and charisma, not everyone was pleased with this development. "Respect for individual human personality has with us reached its lowest point," observed one intellectual in 1921, "and it is delightfully ironical that no nation is so constantly talking about personality as we are. We actually have schools for 'self-expression' 99/929 and 'self-development,' although we seem usually to mean the expression and development of the personality of a successful real estate agent." Another critic bemoaned the slavish attention Americans were starting to pay to entertainers: "It is remarkable how much attention the stage and things pertaining to it are receiving nowadays from the magazines," he grumbled. Only twenty years earlier—during the Culture of Character, that is—such topics would have been considered indecorous; now they had become "such a large part of the life of society that it has become a topic of conversation among all classes." Even T. S. Eliot's famous 1915 poem The Love Song of J. Alfred Prufrock—in which he laments the need to "prepare a face to meet the faces that you meet"—seems a cri de coeur about the 100/929 new demands of self-presentation. While poets of the previous century had wandered lonely as a cloud through the countryside (Wordsworth, in 1802) or repaired in solitude to Walden Pond (Thoreau, in 1845), Eliot's Prufrock mostly worries about being looked at by "eyes that fix you in a formulated phrase" and pin you, wriggling, to a wall. Fast-forward nearly a hundred years, and Prufrock's protest is enshrined in high school syllabi, where it's dutifully memorized, then quickly forgotten, by teens increasingly skilled at shaping their own online and offline personae. These students inhabit a world in which status, income, and self-esteem depend 101/929 more than ever on the ability to meet the demands of the Culture of Personality. The pressure to entertain, to sell ourselves, and never to be visibly anxious keeps ratcheting up. The number of Americans who considered themselves shy increased from 40 percent in the 1970s to 50 percent in the 1990s, probably because we measured ourselves against ever higher standards of fearless self-presentation. "Social anxiety disorder"—which essentially means pathological shyness—is now thought to afflict nearly one in five of us. The most recent version of the Diagnostic and Statistical Manual (DSM-IV), the psychiatrist's bible of mental disorders, considers the fear of public speaking to be a pathology—not an annoyance, not a disadvantage, but a disease—if it interferes with the sufferer's job performance. "It's not enough," one 102/929 senior manager at Eastman Kodak told the author Daniel Goleman, "to be able to sit at your computer excited about a fantastic regression analysis if you're squeamish about presenting those results to an executive group." (Apparently it's OK to be squeamish about doing a regression analysis if you're excited about giving speeches.) But perhaps the best way to take the measure of the twenty-first-century Culture of Personality is to return to the self-help arena. Today, a full century after Dale Carnegie launched that first public-speaking workshop at the YMCA, his best-selling book How to Win Friends and Influence People is a staple of airport bookshelves and business best-seller lists. The Dale Carnegie Institute still offers updated versions of Carnegie's original classes, and the ability to communicate fluidly remains a 103/929 core feature of the curriculum. Toastmasters, the nonprofit organization established in 1924 whose members meet weekly to practice public speaking and whose founder declared that "all talking is selling and all selling involves talking," is still thriving, with more than 12,500 chapters in 113 countries. The promotional video on Toastmasters' website features a skit in which two colleagues, Eduardo and Sheila, sit in the audience at the "Sixth Annual Global Business Conference" as a nervous speaker stumbles through a pitiful presentation. "I'm so glad I'm not him," whispers Eduardo. "You're joking, right?" replies Sheila with a satisfied smile. "Don't you remember last month's sales presentation to those new clients? I thought you were going to faint." 104/929 "I wasn't that bad, was I?" "Oh, you were that bad. Really bad. Worse, even." Eduardo looks suitably ashamed, while the rather insensitive Sheila seems oblivious. "But," says Sheila, "you can fix it. You can do better.... Have you ever heard of Toastmasters?" Sheila, a young and attractive brunette, hauls Eduardo to a Toastmasters meeting. There she volunteers to perform an exercise called "Truth or Lie," in which she's supposed to tell the group of fifteen-odd participants a story about her life, after which they decide whether or not to believe her. "I bet I can fool everyone," she whispers to Eduardo sotto voce as she marches to the podium. She spins an elaborate tale about her years as an opera singer, concluding with her 105/929 poignant decision to give it all up to spend more time with her family. When she's finished, the toastmaster of the evening asks the group whether they believe Sheila's story. All hands in the room go up. The toastmaster turns to Sheila and asks whether it was true. "I can't even carry a tune!" she beams triumphantly. Sheila comes across as disingenuous, but also oddly sympathetic. Like the anxious readers of the 1920s personality guides, she's only trying to get ahead at the office. "There's so much competition in my work environment," she confides to the camera, "that it makes it more important than ever to keep my skills sharp." But what do "sharp skills" look like? Should we become so proficient at selfpresentation that we can dissemble without anyone suspecting? Must we 106/929 learn to stage-manage our voices, gestures, and body language until we can tell—sell—any story we want? These seem venal aspirations, a marker of how far we've come—and not in a good way—since the days of Dale Carnegie's childhood. Dale's parents had high moral standards; they wanted their son to pursue a career in religion or education, not sales. It seems unlikely that they would have approved of a self-improvement technique called "Truth or Lie." Or, for that matter, of Carnegie's best-selling advice on how to get people to admire you and do your bidding. How to Win Friends and Influence People is full of chapter titles like "Making People Glad to Do What You Want" and "How to Make People Like You Instantly." All of which raises the question, how did we go from Character to Personality 107/929 without realizing that we had sacrificed something meaningful along the way?

CHAPTER TWO

The Culture of Personality, a Hundred Years Later

"Are you excited?" cries a young woman named Stacy as I hand her my registration forms. Her honeyed voice rises into one big exclamation point. I nod and smile as brightly as I can. Across the lobby of the Atlanta Convention Center, I hear people shrieking. "What's that noise?" I ask. "They're getting everyone pumped up to go inside!" Stacy enthuses. "That's part of the whole UPW experience." She hands me a purple spiral binder and a laminated nametag to wear around my neck. UNLEASH THE POWER WITHIN, proclaims the binder in big block letters. Welcome to Tony Robbins's entry-level seminar. I've paid $895 in exchange, according to the promotional materials, for 110/929 learning how to be more energetic, gain momentum in my life, and conquer my fears. But the truth is that I'm not here to unleash the power within me (though I'm always happy to pick up a few pointers); I'm here because this seminar is the first stop on my journey to understand the Extrovert Ideal. I've seen Tony Robbins's infomercials—he claims that there's always one airing at any given moment—and he strikes me as one of the more extroverted people on earth. But he's not just any extrovert. He's the king of self-help, with a client roster that has included President Clinton, Tiger Woods, Nelson Mandela, Margaret Thatcher, Princess Diana, Mikhail Gorbachev, Mother Teresa, Serena Williams, Donna Karan—and 50 million other people. And the self-help industry, into which hundreds of thousands of Americans 111/929 pour their hearts, souls, and some $11 billion a year, by definition reveals our conception of the ideal self, the one we aspire to become if only we follow the seven principles of this and the three laws of that. I want to know what this ideal self looks like. Stacy asks if I've brought my meals with me. It seems a strange question: Who carries supper with them from

New York City to Atlanta? She explains that I'll want to refuel at my seat; for the next four days, Friday through Monday, we'll be working fifteen hours a day, 8:00 a.m. to 11:00 p.m., with only one short afternoon break. Tony will be onstage the entire time and I won't want to miss a moment. I look around the lobby. Other people seem to have come prepared—they're strolling toward the hall, cheerfully lugging grocery bags stuffed with 112/929 PowerBars, bananas, and corn chips. I pick up a couple of bruised apples from the snack bar and make my way to the auditorium. Greeters wearing UPW Tshirts and ecstatic smiles line the entrance, springing up and down, fists pumping. You can't get inside without slapping them five. I know, because I try. Inside the vast hall, a phalanx of dancers is warming up the crowd to the Billy Idol song "Mony Mony," amplified by a world-class sound system, magnified on giant Megatron screens flanking the stage. They move in sync like backup dancers in a Britney Spears video, but are dressed like middle managers. The lead performer is a fortysomething balding fellow wearing a white button-down shirt, conservative tie, rolled-up sleeves, and a great-to-meetyou smile. The message seems to be 113/929 that we can all learn to be this exuberant when we get to work every morning. Indeed, the dance moves are simple enough for us to imitate at our seats: jump and clap twice; clap to the left; clap to the right. When the song changes to "Gimme Some Lovin'," many in the audience climb atop their metal folding chairs, where they continue to whoop and clap. I stand somewhat peevishly with arms crossed until I decide that there's nothing to be done but join in and hop up and down along with my seatmates. Eventually the moment we've all been waiting for arrives: Tony Robbins bounds onstage. Already gigantic at six feet seven inches, he looks a hundred feet tall on the Megatron screen. He's movie-star handsome, with a head of thick brown hair, a Pepsodent smile, 114/929 and impossibly defined cheekbones. EXPERIENCE TONY ROBBINS LIVE! the seminar advertisement had promised, and now here he is, dancing with the euphoric crowd. It's about fifty degrees in the hall, but Tony is wearing a short-sleeved polo shirt and shorts. Many in the audience have brought blankets with them, having somehow known that the auditorium would be kept refrigerator-cold, presumably to accommodate Tony's high-octane metabolism. It would take another Ice Age to cool this man off. He's leaping and beaming and managing, somehow, to make eye contact with all 3,800 of us. The greeters jump rapturously in the aisles. Tony opens his arms wide, embracing us all. If Jesus returned to Earth and made his first stop at the Atlanta Convention Center, 115/929 it would be hard to imagine a more jubilant reception. This is true even in the back row where I'm sitting with others who spent only $895 for "general admission," as opposed to $2,500 for a "Diamond Premiere Membership," which gets you a seat up front, as close to Tony as possible. When I bought my ticket over the phone, the account rep advised me that the people in the front rows—where "you're looking directly at Tony for sure" instead of relying on the Megatron—are generally "more successful in life." "Those are the people who have more energy," she advised. "Those are the people who are screaming." I have no way of judging how successful the people next to me are, but they certainly seem thrilled to be here. At the sight of Tony, exquisitely stage-lit to set 116/929 off his expressive face, they cry out and pour into the aisles rock-concert style. Soon enough, I join them. I've always loved to dance, and I have to admit that gyrating en masse to Top 40 classics is an excellent way to pass the time. Unleashed power comes from high energy, according to Tony, and I can see his point. No wonder people travel from far and wide to see him in person (there's a lovely young woman from Ukraine sitting—no, leaping—next to me with a delighted smile). I really must start doing aerobics again when I get back to New York, I decide. When the music finally stops, Tony addresses us in a raspy voice, half 117/929 Muppet, half bedroom-sexy, introducing his theory of "Practical Psychology." The gist of it is that knowledge is useless until it's coupled with action. He has a seductive, fast-talking delivery that Willy Loman would have sighed over. Demonstrating practical psychology in action, Tony instructs us to find a partner and to greet each other as if we feel inferior and scared of social rejection. I team up with a construction worker from downtown Atlanta, and we extend tentative handshakes, looking bashfully at the ground as the song "I Want You to Want Me" plays in the background. Then Tony calls out a series of artfully phrased questions: "Was your breath full or shallow?" "SHALLOW!" yells the audience in unison. 118/929 "Did you hesitate or go straight toward them?" "HESITATE!" "Was there tension in your body or were you relaxed?" "TENSION!" Tony asks us to repeat the exercise, but this time to greet our partners as if the impression we make in the first three to five seconds determines whether they'll do business with us. If they don't, "everyone you care about will die like pigs in hell." I'm startled by Tony's emphasis on business success—this is a seminar about personal power, not sales. Then I remember that Tony is not only a life coach but also a businessman extraordinaire; he started his career in sales and today serves as chairman of seven privately held companies.

BusinessWeek once estimated his income at 119/929 $80 million a year. Now he seems to be trying, with all the force of his mighty personality, to impart his salesman's touch. He wants us not only to feel great but to radiate waves of energy, not just to be liked, but to be well liked; he wants us to know how to sell ourselves. I've already been advised by the Anthony Robbins Companies, via a personalized forty-five-page report generated by an online personality test that I took in preparation for this weekend, that "Susan" should work on her tendency to tell, not sell, her ideas. (The report was written in the third person, as if it was to be reviewed by some imaginary manager evaluating my people skills.) The audience divides into pairs again, enthusiastically introducing themselves and pumping their partners' 120/929 hands. When we're finished, the questions repeat. "Did that feel better, yes or no?" "YES!" "Did you use your body differently, yes or no?" "YES!" "Did you use more muscles in your face, yes or no?" "YES!" "Did you move straight toward them, yes or no?" "YES!" This exercise seems designed to show how our physiological state influences our behavior and emotions, but it also suggests that salesmanship governs even the most neutral interactions. It implies that every encounter is a highstakes game in which we win or lose the other person's favor. It urges us to meet social fear in as extroverted a 121/929 manner as possible. We must be vibrant and confident, we must not seem hesitant, we must smile so that our interlocutors will smile upon us. Taking these steps will make us feel good—and the better we feel, the better we can sell ourselves. Tony seems the perfect person to demonstrate such skills. He strikes me as having a "hyperthymic" temperament—a kind of extroversion-on-steroids characterized, in the words of one psychiatrist, by "exuberant, upbeat, overenergetic, and overconfident lifelong traits" that have been recognized as an asset in business, especially sales. People with these traits often make wonderful company, as Tony does onstage. But what if you admire the hyperthymic among us, but also like your calm and thoughtful self? What if you 122/929 love knowledge for its own sake, not necessarily as a blueprint to action? What if you wish there were more, not fewer, reflective types in the world? Tony seems to have anticipated such questions. "But I'm not an extrovert, you say!" he told us at the start of the seminar. "So? You don't have to be an extrovert to feel alive!" True enough. But it seems, according to Tony, that you'd better act like one if you don't want to flub the sales call and watch your family die like pigs in hell. The evening culminates with the Firewalk, one of the flagship moments of the UPW seminar, in which we're challenged to walk across a ten-foot bed of coals without burning our feet. Many 123/929 people attend UPW because they've heard about the Firewalk and want to try it themselves. The idea is to propel yourself into such a fearless state of mind that you can withstand even 1,200-degree heat. Leading up to that moment, we spend hours practicing Tony's techniques—exercises, dance moves, visualizations. I notice that people in the audience are starting to mimic Tony's every movement and facial expression, including his signature gesture of pumping his arm as if he were pitching a baseball. The evening crescendoes until finally, just before midnight, we march to the parking lot in a torchlit procession, nearly four thousand strong, chanting YES! YES! YES! to the thump of a tribal beat. This seems to electrify my fellow UPWers, but to me this drum-accompanied chant—YES! 124/929 Ba-da-da-da, YES! Dum-dum-dumDUM, YES! Ba-da-da-da—sounds like the sort of thing a Roman general would stage to announce his arrival in the city he's about to sack. The greeters who manned the gates to the auditorium earlier in the day with high fives and bright smiles have morphed into gatekeepers of the Firewalk, arms beckoning toward the bridge of flames. As best I can tell, a successful Firewalk depends not so much on your state of mind as on how thick the soles of your feet happen to be, so I watch from a safe distance. But I seem to be the only one hanging back. Most of the UPWers make it across, whooping as they go. "I did it!" they cry when they get to the other side of the firepit. "I did it!" 125/929 They've entered a Tony Robbins state of mind. But what exactly does this consist of? It is, first and foremost, a superior mind—the antidote to Alfred Adler's inferiority complex. Tony uses the word power rather than superior (we're too sophisticated nowadays to frame our quests for self-improvement in terms of naked social positioning, the way we did at the dawn of the Culture of Personality), but everything about him is an exercise in superiority, from the way he occasionally addresses the audience as "girls and boys," to the stories he tells about his big houses and powerful friends, to the way he towers—literally—over the crowd. His superhuman physical size is an important part of his brand; the title of his best-selling book, Awaken the Giant Within, says it all. 126/929 His intellect is impressive, too. Though he believes university educations are overrated (because they don't teach you about your emotions and your body, he says) and has been slow to write his next book (because no one reads anymore, according to Tony), he's managed to assimilate the work of academic psychologists and package it into one hell of a show, with genuine insights the audience can make their own. Part of Tony's genius lies in the unstated promise that he'll let the audience share his own journey from inferiority to superiority. He wasn't always so grand, he tells us. As a kid, he was a shrimp. Before he got in shape, he was overweight. And before he lived in a castle in Del Mar, California, he rented an apartment so small that he kept his dishes in the bathtub. The implication 127/929 is that we can all get over whatever's keeping us down, that even introverts can learn to walk on coals while belting out a lusty YES. The second part of the Tony state of mind is good-heartedness. He wouldn't inspire so many people if he didn't make them feel that he truly cared about unleashing the power within each of them. When Tony's onstage, you get the sense that he's singing, dancing, and emoting with every ounce of his energy and heart. There are moments, when the crowd is on its feet, singing and dancing in unison, that you can't help but love him, the way many people loved Barack Obama with a kind of shocked delight when they first heard him talk about transcending red and blue. At one point, Tony talks about the different needs people have—for love, certainty, variety, and 128/929 so on. He is motivated by love, he tells us, and we believe him. But there's also this: throughout the seminar, he constantly tries to "upsell" us. He and his sales team use the UPW event, whose attendees have already paid a goodly sum, to market multi-day seminars with even more alluring names and stiffer price tags: Date with Destiny, about $5,000; Mastery University, about $10,000; and the Platinum Partnership, which, for a cool $45,000 a year, buys you and eleven other Platinum Partners the right to go on exotic vacations with Tony. During the afternoon break, Tony lingers onstage with his blond and sweetly beautiful wife, Sage, gazing into her eyes, caressing her hair, murmuring into her ear. I'm happily married, but right now Ken is in New York and I'm here in Atlanta, and even I feel 129/929 lonely as I watch this spectacle. What would it be like if I were single or unhappily partnered? It would "arouse an eager want" in me, just as Dale Carnegie advised salesmen to do with their prospects so many years ago. And sure enough, when the break is over, a lengthy video comes on the megascreen, pitching Tony's relationshipbuilding seminar. In another brilliantly conceived segment, Tony devotes part of the seminar to explaining the financial and emotional benefits of surrounding oneself with the right "peer group"—after which a staffer begins a sales pitch for the $45,000 Platinum program. Those who purchase one of the twelve spots will join the "ultimate peer group," we are told—the "cream of the crop," the "elite of the elite of the elite." 130/929 I can't help but wonder why none of the other UPWers seem to mind, or even to notice, these upselling techniques. By now many of them have shopping bags at their feet, full of stuff they bought out in the lobby—DVDs, books, even eight-by-ten glossies of Tony himself, ready for framing. But the thing about Tony—and what draws people to buy his products—is that like any good salesman, he believes in what he's pitching. He apparently sees no contradiction between wanting the best for people and wanting to live in a mansion. He persuades us that he's using his sales skills not only for personal gain but also to help as many of us as he can reach. Indeed, one very thoughtful introvert I know, a successful salesman who gives sales training seminars of his own, swears that Tony Robbins not only improved his business 131/929 but also made him a better person. When he started attending events like UPW, he says, he focused on who he wanted to become, and now, when he delivers his own seminars, he is that person. "Tony gives me energy," he says, "and now I can create energy for other people when I'm onstage." At the onset of the Culture of Personality, we were urged to develop an extroverted personality for frankly selfish reasons—as a way of outshining the crowd in a newly anonymous and competitive society. But nowadays we tend to think that becoming more extroverted not only makes us more successful, but also makes us better people. We see 132/929 salesmanship as a way of sharing one's gifts with the world. This is why Tony's zeal to sell to and be adulated by thousands of people at once is seen not as narcissism or hucksterism, but as leadership of the highest order. If Abraham Lincoln was the embodiment of virtue during the Culture of Character, then Tony Robbins is his counterpart during the Culture of Personality. Indeed, when Tony mentions that he once thought of running for president of the United States, the audience erupts in loud cheers. But does it always make sense to equate leadership with hyper-extroversion? To find out, I visited Harvard Business School, an institution that prides itself on its ability to identify and train some of the most prominent business and political leaders of our time. 133/929 The Myth of Charismatic Leadership: Harvard Business School and Beyond The first thing I notice about the Harvard Business School campus is the way people walk. No one ambles, strolls, or lingers. They stride, full of forward momentum. It's crisp and autumnal the week I visit, and the students' bodies seem to vibrate with September electricity as they advance across campus. When they cross each other's paths they don't merely nod—they exchange animated greetings, inquiring about this one's summer with J. P. Morgan or that one's trek in the Himalayas. They behave the same way inside the social hothouse of the Spangler Center, the sumptuously decorated student center. Spangler has floor-to-ceiling silk curtains in sea-foam green, rich leather sofas, giant Samsung high-definition 134/929 TVs silently broadcasting campus news, and soaring ceilings festooned with high-wattage chandeliers. The tables and sofas are clustered mostly on the perimeter of the room, forming a brightly lit center catwalk down which the students breezily parade, seemingly unaware that all eyes are on them. I admire their nonchalance. The students are even better turned out than their surroundings, if such a thing is possible. No one is more than five pounds overweight or has bad skin or wears odd accessories. The women are a cross between Head Cheerleader and Most Likely to Succeed. They wear fitted jeans, filmy blouses, and highheeled peekaboo-toed shoes that make a pleasing clickety–clack on Spangler's polished wood floors. Some parade like fashion models, except that they're social and beaming instead of aloof and 135/929 impassive. The men are clean-cut and athletic; they look like people who expect to be in charge, but in a friendly, Eagle Scout sort of way. I have the feeling that if you asked one of them for driving directions, he'd greet you with a can-do smile and throw himself into the task of helping you to your destination—whether or not he knew the way. I sit down next to a couple of students who are in the middle of planning a road trip—HBS students are forever coordinating pub crawls and parties, or describing an extreme-travel junket they've just come back from. When they ask what brings me to campus, I say that I'm conducting interviews for a book about introversion and extroversion. I don't tell them that a friend of mine, himself an HBS grad, once called the place the "Spiritual 136/929 Capital of Extroversion." But it turns out that I don't have to tell them. "Good luck finding an introvert around here," says one. "This school is predicated on extroversion," adds the other. "Your grades and social status depend on it. It's just the norm here. Everyone around you is speaking up and being social and going out." "Isn't there anyone on the quieter side?" I ask. They look at me curiously. "I couldn't tell you," says the first student dismissively. Harvard Business School is not, by any measure, an ordinary place. Founded in 1908, just when Dale Carnegie hit the 137/929 road as a traveling salesman and only three years before he taught his first class in public speaking, the school sees itself as "educating leaders who make a difference in the world." President George W. Bush is a graduate, as are an impressive collection of World Bank presidents,

U.S. Treasury secretaries, New York City mayors, CEOs of companies like General Electric, Goldman Sachs, Procter & Gamble, and, more notoriously, Jeffrey Skilling, the villain of the Enron scandal. Between 2004 and 2006, 20 percent of the top three executives at the Fortune 500 companies were HBS grads. HBS grads likely have influenced your life in ways you're not aware of. They have decided who should go to war and when; they have resolved the fate of Detroit's auto industry; they play leading roles in just about every crisis 138/929 to shake Wall Street, Main Street, and Pennsylvania Avenue. If you work in corporate America, there's a good chance that Harvard Business School grads have shaped your everyday life, too, weighing in on how much privacy you need in your workspace, how many team-building sessions you need to attend per year, and whether creativity is best achieved through brainstorming or solitude. Given the scope of their influence, it's worth taking a look at who enrolls here—and what they value by the time they graduate. The student who wishes me luck in finding an introvert at HBS no doubt believes that there are none to be found. But clearly he doesn't know his first-year classmate Don Chen. I first meet Don in Spangler, where he's seated only a few couches away from the road-trip planners. He comes across 139/929 as a typical HBS student, tall, with gracious manners, prominent cheekbones, a winsome smile, and a fashionably choppy, surfer-dude haircut. He'd like to find a job in private equity when he graduates. But talk to Don for a while and you'll notice that his voice is softer than those of his classmates, his head ever so slightly cocked, his grin a little tentative. Don is "a bitter introvert," as he cheerfully puts it—bitter because the more time he spends at HBS, the more convinced he becomes that he'd better change his ways. Don likes having a lot of time to himself, but that's not much of an option at HBS. His day begins early in the morning, when he meets for an hour and a half with his "Learning Team"—a preassigned study group in which participation is mandatory (students at HBS practically go to the bathroom in 140/929 teams). He spends the rest of the morning in class, where ninety students sit together in a wood-paneled, U-shaped amphitheater with stadium seating. The professor usually kicks off by directing a student to describe the case study of the day, which is based on a real-life business scenario—say, a CEO who's considering changing her company's salary structure. The figure at the heart of the case study, in this case the CEO, is referred to as the "protagonist." If you were the protagonist, the professor asks—and soon you will be, is the implication—what would you do? The essence of the HBS education is that leaders have to act confidently and make decisions in the face of incomplete information. The teaching method plays with an age-old question: If you don't have all the facts—and often you won't—should you wait to act until 141/929 you've collected as much data as possible? Or, by hesitating, do you risk losing others' trust and your own momentum? The answer isn't obvious. If you speak firmly on the basis of bad information, you can lead your people into disaster. But if you exude uncertainty, then morale suffers, funders won't invest, and your organization can collapse. The HBS teaching method implicitly comes down on the side of certainty. The CEO may not know the best way forward, but she has to act anyway. The HBS students, in turn, are expected to opine. Ideally, the student who was just cold-called has already discussed the case study with his Learning Team, so he's ready to hold forth on the protagonist's best moves. After he finishes, the professor encourages other students to offer their own views. Half of the 142/929 students' grade, and a much larger percentage of their social status, is based on whether they throw themselves into this fray. If a student talks often and forcefully, then he's a player; if he doesn't, he's on the margins. Many of the students adapt easily to this system. But not Don. He has trouble elbowing his way into class discussions; in some classes he barely speaks at all. He prefers to contribute only when he believes he has something insightful to add, or honestto-God disagrees with someone. This sounds reasonable, but Don feels as if he should be more comfortable talking just so he can fill up his share of available airtime. Don's HBS friends, who tend to be thoughtful, reflective types like him, spend a lot of time talking about talking in class. How much class 143/929 participation is too much? How little is too little? When does publicly disagreeing with a classmate constitute healthy debate, and when does it seem competitive and judgmental? One of Don's friends is worried because her professor sent around an e-mail saying that anyone with real-world experience on the day's case study should let him know in advance. She's sure that the professor's announcement was an effort to limit stupid remarks like the one she made in class last week. Another worries that he's not loud enough. "I just have a naturally soft voice," he says, "so when my voice sounds normal to others, I feel like I'm shouting. I have to work on it." The school also tries hard to turn quiet students into talkers. The professors have their own "Learning Teams," in which they egg each other on with techniques to draw out reticent 144/929 students. When students fail to speak up in class, it's seen not only as their own deficit but also as their professor's. "If someone doesn't speak by the end of the semester, it's problematic," Professor Michel Anteby told me. "It means I didn't do a good job." The school even hosts live informational sessions and web pages on how to be a good class participator. Don's friends earnestly reel off the tips they remember best. "Speak with conviction. Even if you believe something only fifty-five percent, say it as if you believe it a hundred percent." "If you're preparing alone for class, then you're doing it wrong. Nothing at HBS is intended to be done alone." "Don't think about the perfect answer. It's better to get out there and say 145/929 something than to never get your voice in." The school newspaper, The Harbus, also dispenses advice, featuring articles with titles like "How to Think and Speak Well—On the Spot!," "Developing Your Stage Presence," and "Arrogant or Simply Confident?" These imperatives extend beyond the classroom. After class, most people eat lunch at the Spangler dining hall, which one grad describes as "more like high school than high school." And every day, Don wrestles with himself. Should he go back to his apartment and recharge over a quiet lunch, as he longs to do, or join his classmates? Even if he forces himself to go to Spangler, it's not as if the social pressure will end there. As the day wears on, there will be more such dilemmas. Attend the late-afternoon happy hours? Head out for a late, 146/929 rowdy evening? Students at HBS go out in big groups several nights a week, says Don. Participation isn't mandatory, but it feels as if it is to those who don't thrive on group activities. "Socializing here is an extreme sport," one of Don's friends tells me. "People go out all the time. If you don't go out one night, the next day people will ask, 'Where were you?' I go out at night like it's my job." Don has noticed that the people who organize social events—happy hours, dinners, drinking fests—are at the top of the social hierarchy. "The professors tell us that our classmates are the people who will go to our weddings," says Don. "If you leave HBS without having built an extensive social network, it's like you failed your HBS experience." By the time Don falls into bed at night, he's exhausted. And sometimes 147/ 929 he wonders why, exactly, he should have to work so hard at being outgoing. Don is Chinese-American, and recently he worked a summer job in China. He was struck by how different the social norms were, and how much more comfortable he felt. In China there was more emphasis on listening, on asking questions rather than holding forth, on putting others' needs first. In the United States, he feels, conversation is about how effective you are at turning your experiences into stories, whereas a Chinese person might be concerned with taking up too much of the other person's time with inconsequential information. "That summer, I said to myself, 'Now I know why these are my people,' " he says. But that was China, this is Cambridge, Massachusetts. And if one 148/929 judges HBS by how well it prepares students for the "real world," it seems to be doing an excellent job. After all, Don Chen will graduate into a business culture in which verbal fluency and sociability are the two most important predictors of success, according to a Stanford Business School study. It's a world in which a middle manager at GE once told me that "people here don't even want to meet with you if you don't have a PowerPoint and a 'pitch' for them. Even if you're just making a recommendation to your colleague, you can't sit down in someone's office and tell them what you think. You have to make a presentation, with pros and cons and a 'takeaway box.' " Unless they're self-employed or able to telecommute, many adults work in offices where they must take care to glide down the corridors greeting their 149/929 colleagues warmly and confidently. "The business world," says a 2006 article from the Wharton Program for Working Professionals, "is filled with office environments similar to one described by an Atlanta area corporate trainer: 'Here everyone knows that it's important to be an extrovert and troublesome to be an introvert. So people work real hard at looking like extroverts, whether that's comfortable or not. It's like making sure you drink the same single-malt scotch the CEO drinks and that you work out at the right health club.' " Even businesses that employ many artists, designers, and other imaginative types often display a preference for extroversion. "We want to attract creative people," the director of human resources at a major media company told me. When I asked what she meant by 150/929 "creative," she answered without missing a beat. "You have to be outgoing, fun, and jazzed up to work here." Contemporary ads aimed at businesspeople would give the Williams Luxury Shaving Cream ads of yesteryear a run for their money. One line of TV commercials that ran on CNBC, the cable business channel, featured an office worker losing out on a plum assignment. BOSS TO TED AND ALICE. Ted, I'm sending Alice to the sales conference because she thinks faster on her feet than you. TED. (speechless) ... BOSS. So, Alice, we'll send you on Thursday— TED. She does not! 151/929 Other ads explicitly sell their products as extroversion-enhancers. In 2000, Amtrak encouraged travelers to "DEPART FROM YOUR INHIBITIONS." Nike became a prominent brand partly on the strength of its "Just Do It" campaign. And in 1999 and 2000, a series of ads for the psychotropic drug Paxil promised to cure the extreme shyness known as "social anxiety disorder" by offering Cinderella stories of personality transformation. One Paxil ad showed a welldressed executive shaking hands over a business deal. "I can taste success," read the caption. Another showed what happens without the drug: a businessman alone in his office, his forehead resting dejectedly on a clenched fist. "I should have joined in more often," it read. 152/929 Yet even at Harvard Business School there are signs that something might be wrong with a leadership style that values quick and assertive answers over quiet, slow decision-making. Every autumn the incoming class participates in an elaborate role-playing game called the Subarctic Survival Situation. "It is approximately 2:30 p.m., October 5," the students are told, "and you have just crash-landed in a float plane on the east shore of Laura Lake in the subarctic region of the northern Quebec-Newfoundland border." The students are divided into small groups and asked to imagine that their group has salvaged fifteen items from the plane—a compass, sleeping bag, axe, and so on. Then they're told to rank 153/929 them in order of importance to the group's survival. First the students rank the items individually; then they do so as a team. Next they score those rankings against an expert's to see how well they did. Finally they watch a videotape of their team's discussions to see what went right—or wrong. The point of the exercise is to teach group synergy. Successful synergy means a higher ranking for the team than for its individual members. The group fails when any of its members has a better ranking than the overall team. And failure is exactly what can happen when students prize assertiveness too highly. One of Don's classmates was in a group lucky to include a young man with extensive experience in the northern backwoods. He had a lot of good ideas about how to rank the fifteen 154/929 salvaged items. But his group didn't listen, because he expressed his views too quietly. "Our action plan hinged on what the most vocal people suggested," recalls the classmate. "When the less vocal people put out ideas, those ideas were discarded. The ideas that were rejected would have kept us alive and out of trouble, but they were dismissed because of the conviction with which the more vocal people suggested their ideas. Afterwards they played us back the videotape, and it was so embarrassing." The Subarctic Survival Situation may sound like a harmless game played inside the ivory tower, but if you think of meetings you've attended, you can probably recall a time—plenty of times—when the opinion of the most dynamic or talkative person prevailed 155/929 to the detriment of all. Perhaps it was a low-stakes situation—your PTA, say, deciding whether to meet on Monday or Tuesday nights. But maybe it was important: an emergency meeting of Enron's top brass, considering whether or not to disclose questionable accounting practices. (See chapter 7 for more on Enron.) Or a jury deliberating whether or not to send a single mother to jail. I discussed the Subarctic Survival Situation with HBS professor Quinn Mills, an expert on leadership styles. Mills is a courteous man dressed, on the day we met, in a pinstriped suit and yellow polka-dot tie. He has a sonorous voice, and uses it skillfully. The HBS method "presumes that leaders should be vocal," he told me flat out, "and in my view that's part of reality." 156/929 But Mills also pointed to the common phenomenon known as the "winner's curse," in which two companies bid competitively to acquire a third, until the price climbs so high that it becomes less an economic activity than a war of egos. The winning bidders will be damned if they'll let their opponents get the prize, so they buy the target company at an inflated price. "It tends to be the assertive people who carry the day in these kinds of things," says Mills. "You see this all the time. People ask, 'How did this happen, how did we pay so much?' Usually it's said that they were carried away by the situation, but that's not right. Usually they're carried away by people who are assertive and domineering. The risk with our students is that they're very good at getting their way. But that doesn't mean they're going the right way." 157/929 If we assume that quiet and loud people have roughly the same number of good (and bad) ideas, then we should worry if the louder and more forceful people always carry the day. This would mean that an awful lot of bad ideas prevail while good ones get squashed. Yet studies in group dynamics suggest that this is exactly what happens. We perceive talkers as smarter than quiet types—even though gradepoint averages and SAT and intelligence test scores reveal this perception to be inaccurate. In one experiment in which two strangers met over the phone, those who spoke more were considered more intelligent, better looking, and more likable. We also see talkers as leaders. The more a person talks, the more other group members direct their attention to him, which means that he becomes increasingly 158/929 powerful as a meeting goes on. It also helps to speak fast; we rate quick talkers as more capable and appealing than slow talkers. All of this would be fine if more talking were correlated with greater insight, but research suggests that there's no such link. In one study, groups of college students were asked to solve math problems together and then to rate one another's intelligence and judgment. The students who spoke first and most often were consistently given the highest ratings, even though their suggestions (and math SAT scores) were no better than those of the less talkative students. These same students were given similarly high ratings for their creativity and analytical powers during a separate exercise to develop a business strategy for a start-up company. 159/929 A well-known study out of UC Berkeley by organizational behavior professor Philip Tetlock found that television pundits—that is, people who earn their livings by holding forth confidently on the basis of limited information—make worse predictions about political and economic trends than they would by random chance. And the very worst prognosticators tend to be the most famous and the most confident—the very ones who would be considered natural leaders in an HBS classroom. The U.S. Army has a name for a similar phenomenon: "the Bus to Abilene." "Any army officer can tell you what that means," Colonel (Ret.) Stephen J. Gerras, a professor of behavioral sciences at the U.S. Army War College, told Yale Alumni Magazine in 2008. "It's about a family sitting on a porch in Texas on a hot summer day, and 160/929 somebody says, 'I'm bored. Why don't we go to Abilene?' When they get to Abilene, somebody says, 'You know, I didn't really want to go.' And the next person says, 'I didn't want to go—I thought you wanted to go,' and so on. Whenever you're in an army group and somebody says, 'I think we're all getting on the bus to Abilene here,' that is a red flag. You can stop a conversation with it. It is a very powerful artifact of our culture." The "Bus to Abilene" anecdote reveals our tendency to follow those who initiate action—any action. We are similarly inclined to empower dynamic speakers. One highly successful venture capitalist who is regularly pitched by young entrepreneurs told me how frustrated he is by his colleagues' failure to distinguish between good presentation skills and true leadership ability. "I 161/929 worry that there are people who are put in positions of authority because they're good talkers, but they don't have good ideas," he said. "It's so easy to confuse schmoozing ability with talent. Someone seems like a good presenter, easy to get along with, and those traits are rewarded. Well, why is that? They're valuable traits, but we put too much of a premium on presenting and not enough on substance and critical thinking." In his book Iconoclast, the neuroeconomist Gregory Berns explores what happens when companies rely too heavily on presentation skills to weed out good ideas from nonstarters. He describes a software company called RiteSolutions that successfully asks employees to share ideas through an online "idea market," as a way of focusing on substance rather than style.

Joe Marino, 162/929 president of Rite-Solutions, and Jim Lavoie, CEO of the company, created this system as a reaction to problems they'd experienced elsewhere. "In my old company," Lavoie told Berns, "if you had a great idea, we would tell you, 'OK, we'll make an appointment for you to address the murder board' "—a group of people charged with vetting new ideas. Marino described what happened next: Some technical guy comes in with a good idea. Of course questions are asked of that person that they don't know. Like, "How big's the market? What's your marketing approach? What's your business plan for this? What's the product going to cost?" It's embarrassing. Most people can't answer those kinds of questions. The people who made it through these 163/929 boards were not the people with the best ideas. They were the best presenters. Contrary to the Harvard Business School model of vocal leadership, the ranks of effective CEOs turn out to be filled with introverts, including Charles Schwab; Bill Gates; Brenda Barnes, CEO of Sara Lee; and James Copeland, former CEO of Deloitte Touche Tohmatsu. "Among the most effective leaders I have encountered and worked with in half a century," the management guru Peter Drucker has written, "some locked themselves into their office and others were ultra-gregarious. Some were quick and impulsive, while others studied the situation and took forever to come to a decision.... The one and only personality trait the effective ones I have encountered did 164/929 have in common was something they did not have: they had little or no 'charisma' and little use either for the term or what it signifies." Supporting Drucker's claim, Brigham Young University management professor Bradley Agle studied the CEOs of 128 major companies and found that those considered charismatic by their top executives had bigger salaries but not better corporate performance. We tend to overestimate how outgoing leaders need to be. "Most leading in a corporation is done in small meetings and it's done at a distance, through written and video communications," Professor Mills told me. "It's not done in front of big groups. You have to be able to do some of that; you can't be a leader of a corporation and walk into a room full of analysts and turn white with fear and leave. But you don't have 165/929 to do a whole lot of it. I've known a lot of leaders of corporations who are highly introspective and who really have to make themselves work to do the public stuff." Mills points to Lou Gerstner, the legendary chairman of IBM. "He went to school here," he says. "I don't know how he'd characterize himself. He has to give big speeches, and he does, and he looks calm. But my sense is that he's dramatically more comfortable in small groups. Many of these guys are, actually. Not all of them. But an awful lot of them." Indeed, according to a famous study by the influential management theorist Jim Collins, many of the best-performing companies of the late twentieth century were run by what he calls "Level 5 Leaders." These exceptional CEOs were known not for their flash or 166/929 charisma but for extreme humility coupled with intense professional will. In his influential book Good to Great, Collins tells the story of Darwin Smith, who in his twenty years as head of Kimberly-Clark turned it into the leading paper company in the world and generated stock returns more than four times higher than the market average. Smith was a shy and mild-mannered man who wore J.C. Penney suits and nerdy black-rimmed glasses, and spent his vacations puttering around his Wisconsin farm by himself. Asked by a Wall Street Journal reporter to describe his management style, Smith stared back for an uncomfortably long time and answered with a single word: "Eccentric." But his soft demeanor concealed a fierce resolve. Soon after being appointed CEO, Smith made a dramatic decision to sell the mills that produced 167/ 929 the company's core business of coated paper and invest instead in the consumer-paper-products industry, which he believed had better economics and a brighter future. Everyone said this was a huge mistake, and Wall Street downgraded Kimberly-Clark's stock. But Smith, unmoved by the crowd, did what he thought was right. As a result, the company grew stronger and soon outpaced its rivals. Asked later about his strategy, Smith replied that he never stopped trying to become qualified for the job. Collins hadn't set out to make a point about quiet leadership. When he started his research, all he wanted to know was what characteristics made a company outperform its competition. He selected eleven standout companies to research in depth. Initially he ignored the question of leadership altogether, because 168/929 he wanted to avoid simplistic answers. But when he analyzed what the highest-performing companies had in common, the nature of their CEOs jumped out at him. Every single one of them was led by an unassuming man like Darwin Smith. Those who worked with these leaders tended to describe them with the following words: quiet, humble, modest, reserved, shy, gracious, mild-mannered, self-effacing, understated. The lesson, says Collins, is clear. We don't need giant personalities to transform companies. We need leaders who build not their own egos but the institutions they run. 169/929 So what do introverted leaders do differently from—and sometimes better than—extroverts? One answer comes from the work of Wharton management professor Adam

Grant, who has spent considerable time consulting with Fortune 500 executives and military leaders—from Google to the U.S. Army and Navy. When we first spoke, Grant was teaching at the Ross School of Business at the University of Michigan, where he'd become convinced that the existing research, which showed a correlation between extroversion and leadership, didn't tell the whole story. Grant told me about a wing commander in the U.S. Air Force—one rank below general, in command of thousands of people, charged with protecting a high-security missile base—who was one of the most classically 170/929 introverted people, as well as one of the finest leaders, Grant had ever met. This man lost focus when he interacted too much with people, so he carved out time for thinking and recharging. He spoke quietly, without much variation in his vocal inflections or facial expressions. He was more interested in listening and gathering information than in asserting his opinion or dominating a conversation. He was also widely admired; when he spoke, everyone listened. This was not necessarily remarkable—if you're at the top of the military hierarchy, people are supposed to listen to you. But in the case of this commander, says Grant, people respected not just his formal authority, but also the way he led: by supporting his employees' efforts to take the initiative. He gave subordinates input into key decisions, 171/929 implementing the ideas that made sense, while making it clear that he had the final authority. He wasn't concerned with getting credit or even with being in charge; he simply assigned work to those who could perform it best. This meant delegating some of his most interesting, meaningful, and important tasks—work that other leaders would have kept for themselves. Why did the research not reflect the talents of people like the wing commander? Grant thought he knew what the problem was. First, when he looked closely at the existing studies on personality and leadership, he found that the correlation between extroversion and leadership was modest. Second, these studies were often based on people's perceptions of who made a good leader, as opposed to actual 172/929 results. And personal opinions are often a simple reflection of cultural bias. But most intriguing to Grant was that the existing research didn't differentiate among the various kinds of situations a leader might face. It might be that certain organizations or contexts were better suited to introverted leadership styles, he thought, and others to extroverted approaches, but the studies didn't make such distinctions. Grant had a theory about which kinds of circumstances would call for introverted leadership. His hypothesis was that extroverted leaders enhance group performance when employees are passive, but that introverted leaders are more effective with proactive employees. To test his idea, he and two colleagues, professors Francesca Gino of Harvard Business School and David Hofman of the Kenan-Flagler Business 173/929 School at the University of North Carolina, carried out a pair of studies of their own. In the first study, Grant and his colleagues analyzed data from one of the five biggest pizza chains in the United States. They discovered that the weekly profits of the stores managed by extroverts were 16 percent higher than the profits of those led by introverts—but only when the employees were passive types who tended to do their job without exercising initiative. Introverted leaders had the exact opposite results. When they worked with employees who actively tried to improve work procedures, their stores outperformed those led by extroverts by more than 14 percent. In the second study, Grant's team divided 163 college students into competing teams charged with folding as many 174/929 T-shirts as possible in ten minutes. Unbeknownst to the participants, each team included two actors. In some teams, the two actors acted passively, following the leader's instructions. In other teams, one of the actors said, "I wonder if there's a more efficient way to do this." The other actor replied that he had a friend from Japan who had a faster way to fold shirts. "It might take a minute or two to teach you," the actor told the leader, "but do we want to try it?" The results were striking. The introverted leaders were 20 percent more likely to follow the suggestion—and their teams had 24 percent better results than the teams of the extroverted leaders. When the followers were not proactive, though—when they simply did as the leader instructed without suggesting their own shirt-folding 175/929 methods—the teams led by extroverts outperformed those led by the introverts by 22 percent. Why did these leaders' effectiveness turn on whether their employees were passive or proactive? Grant says it makes sense that introverts are uniquely good at leading initiativetakers. Because of their inclination to listen to others and lack of interest in dominating social situations, introverts are more likely to hear and implement suggestions. Having benefited from the talents of their followers, they are then likely to motivate them to be even more proactive. Introverted leaders create a virtuous circle of proactivity, in other words. In the T-shirt-folding study, the team members reported perceiving the introverted leaders as more open and receptive to their ideas, 176/929 which motivated them to work harder and to fold more shirts. Extroverts, on the other hand, can be so intent on putting their own stamp on events that they risk losing others' good ideas along the way and allowing workers to lapse into passivity. "Often the leaders end up doing a lot of the talking," says Francesca Gino, "and not listening to any of the ideas that the followers are trying to provide." But with their natural ability to inspire, extroverted leaders are better at getting results from more passive workers. This line of research is still in its infancy. But under the auspices of Grant—an especially proactive fellow himself—it may grow quickly. (One of his colleagues has described Grant as the kind of person who "can make things happen twenty-eight minutes before they're scheduled to begin.") Grant 177/929 is especially excited about the implications of these findings because proactive employees who take advantage of opportunities in a fast-moving, 24/7 business environment, without waiting for a leader to tell them what to do, are increasingly vital to organizational success. To understand how to maximize these employees' contributions is an important tool for all leaders. It's also important for companies to groom listeners as well as talkers for leadership roles. The popular press, says Grant, is full of suggestions that introverted leaders practice their public speaking skills and smile more. But Grant's research suggests that in at least one important regard—encouraging employees to take initiative—introverted leaders would do well to go on doing what they do naturally. Extroverted leaders, on the 178/929 other hand, "may wish to adopt a more reserved, quiet style," Grant writes. They may want to learn to sit down so that others might stand up. Which is just what a woman named Rosa Parks did naturally. For years before the day in December 1955 when Rosa Parks refused to give up her seat on a Montgomery bus, she worked behind the scenes for the NAACP, even receiving training in nonviolent resistance. Many things had inspired her political commitment. The time the Ku Klux Klan marched in front of her childhood house. The time her brother, a private in the U.S. Army who'd saved the lives of white soldiers, came home from World War II only to 179/929 be spat upon. The time a black eighteen-year-old delivery boy was framed for rape and sent to the electric chair. Parks organized NAACP records, kept track of membership payments, read to little kids in her neighborhood. She was diligent and honorable, but no one thought of her as a leader. Parks, it seemed, was more of a foot soldier. Not many people know that twelve years before her showdown with the Montgomery bus driver, she'd had another encounter with the same man, possibly on the very same bus. It was a November afternoon in 1943, and Parks had entered through the front door of the bus because the back was too crowded. The driver, a well-known bigot named James Blake, told her to use the rear and started to push her off the bus. Parks asked him not to touch her. She would leave on her own, she said 180/929 quietly. "Get off my bus," Blake sputtered in response. Parks complied, but not before deliberately dropping her purse on her way out and sitting on a "white" seat as she picked it up. "Intuitively, she had engaged in an act of passive resistance, a precept named by Leo Tolstoy and embraced by Mahatma Gandhi," writes the historian Douglas Brinkley in a wonderful biography of Parks. It was more than a decade before King popularized the idea of nonviolence and long before Parks's own training in civil disobedience, but, Brinkley writes, "such principles were a perfect match for her own personality." Parks was so disgusted by Blake that she refused to ride his bus for the next twelve years. On the day she finally did, the day that turned her into the "Mother of the Civil Rights Movement," 181/929 she got back on that bus, according to Brinkley, only out of sheer absentmindedness. Parks's actions that day were brave and singular, but it was in the legal fallout that her quiet strength truly shone. Local civil rights leaders sought her out as a test case to challenge the city's bus laws, pressing her to file a lawsuit. This was no small decision. Parks had a sickly mother who depended on her; to sue would mean losing her job and her husband's. It would mean running the very real risk of being lynched from "the tallest telephone pole in town," as her husband and mother put it. "Rosa, the white folks will kill you," pleaded her husband. "It was one thing to be arrested for an isolated bus incident," writes Brinkley; "it was quite another, as historian Taylor Branch would put it, 182/929 to 'reenter that forbidden zone by choice.' " But because of her nature, Parks was the perfect plaintiff. Not only because she was a devout Christian, not only because she was an upstanding citizen, but also because she was gentle. "They've messed with the wrong one now!" the boycotters would declare as they traipsed miles to work and school. The phrase became a rallying cry. Its power lay in how paradoxical it was. Usually such a phrase implies that you've messed with a local heavy, with some bullying giant. But it was Parks's quiet strength that made her unassailable. "The slogan served as a reminder that the woman who had inspired the boycott was the sort of soft-spoken martyr God would not abandon," writes Brinkley. 183/929 Parks took her time coming to a decision, but ultimately agreed to sue. She also lent her presence at a rally held on the evening of her trial, the night when a young Martin Luther King Jr., the head of the brand-new Montgomery Improvement Association, roused all of Montgomery's black community to boycott the buses. "Since it had to happen," King told the crowd, "I'm happy it happened to a person like Rosa Parks, for nobody can doubt the boundless outreach of her integrity. Nobody can doubt the height of her character. Mrs. Parks is unassuming, and yet there is integrity and character there." Later that year Parks agreed to go on a fund-raising speaking tour with King and other civil rights leaders. She suffered insomnia, ulcers, and homesickness along the way. She met her idol, Eleanor Roosevelt, who wrote of 184/929 their encounter in her newspaper column: "She is a very quiet, gentle person and it is difficult to imagine how she ever could take such a positive and independent stand." When the boycott finally ended, over a year later, the buses integrated by decree of the Supreme Court, Parks was overlooked by the press. The New York Times ran two front-page stories that celebrated King but didn't mention her. Other papers photographed the boycott leaders sitting in front of buses, but Parks was not invited to sit for these pictures. She didn't mind. On the day the buses were integrated, she preferred to stay home and take care of her mother. 185/929 Parks's story is a vivid reminder that we have been graced with limelightavoiding leaders throughout history. Moses, for example, was not, according to some interpretations of his story, the brash, talkative type who would organize road trips and hold forth in a classroom at Harvard Business School. On the contrary, by today's standards he was dreadfully timid. He spoke with a stutter and considered himself inarticulate. The book of Numbers describes him as "very meek, above all the men which were upon the face of the earth." When God first appeared to him in the form of a burning bush, Moses was employed as a shepherd by his fatherin-law; he wasn't even ambitious enough to own his own sheep. And when God revealed to Moses his role as liberator of the Jews, did Moses leap at the opportunity? Send someone else to 186/929 do it, he said. "Who am I, that I should go to Pharaoh?" he pleaded. "I have never been eloquent. I am slow of speech and tongue." It was only when God paired him up with his extroverted brother Aaron that Moses agreed to take on the assignment. Moses would be the speechwriter, the behind-the-scenes guy, the Cyrano de Bergerac; Aaron would be the public face of the operation. "It will be as if he were your mouth," said God, "and as if you were God to him." Complemented by Aaron, Moses led the Jews from Egypt, provided for them in the desert for the next forty years, and brought the Ten Commandments down from Mount Sinai. And he did all this using strengths that are classically associated with introversion: climbing a mountain in search of wisdom and 187/929 writing down carefully, on two stone tablets, everything he learned there. We tend to write Moses' true personality out of the Exodus story. (Cecil B. DeMille's classic, The Ten Commandments, portrays him as a swashbuckling figure who does all the talking, with no help from Aaron.) We don't ask why God chose as his prophet a stutterer with a public speaking phobia. But we should. The book of Exodus is short on explication, but its stories suggest that introversion plays yin to the yang of extroversion; that the medium is not always the message; and that people followed Moses because his words were thoughtful, not because he spoke them well. 188/929 If Parks spoke through her actions, and if Moses spoke through his brother Aaron, today another type of introverted leader speaks using the Internet. In his book The Tipping Point, Malcolm Gladwell explores the influence of "Connectors"—people who have a "special gift for bringing the world together" and "an instinctive and natural gift for making social connections." He describes a "classic Connector" named Roger Horchow, a charming and successful businessman and backer of Broadway hits such as Les Misérables, who "collects people the same way others collect stamps." "If you sat next to Roger Horchow on a plane ride across the Atlantic," writes Gladwell, "he would start talking as the plane taxied to the runway, you would be laughing by the time the seatbelt sign was turned off, 189/929 and when you landed at the other end you'd wonder where the time went." We generally think of Connectors in just the way that Gladwell describes Horchow: chatty, outgoing, spellbinding even. But consider for a moment a modest, cerebral man named Craig Newmark. Short, balding, and bespectacled, Newmark was a systems engineer for seventeen years at IBM. Before that, he had consuming interests in dinosaurs, chess, and physics. If you sat next to him on a plane, he'd probably keep his nose buried in a book. Yet Newmark also happens to be the founder and majority owner of Craigslist, the eponymous website that—well—connects people with each other. As of May 28, 2011, Craigslist was the seventh-largest English language website in the world. Its users in over 700 cities in seventy countries find 190/929 jobs, dates, and even kidney donors on Newmark's site. They join singing groups. They read one another's haikus. They confess their affairs. Newmark describes the site not as a business but as a public commons. "Connecting people to fix the world over time is the deepest spiritual value you can have," Newmark has said. After Hurricane Katrina, Craigslist helped stranded families find new homes. During the New York City transit strike of 2005, Craigslist was the goto place for ride-share listings. "Yet another crisis, and Craigslist commands the community," wrote one blogger about Craigslist's role in the strike. "How come Craig organically can touch lives on so many personal levels—and Craig's users can touch each other's lives on so many levels?" 191/929 Here's one answer: social media has made new forms of leadership possible for scores of people who don't fit the Harvard Business School mold. On August 10, 2008, Guy Kawasaki, the best-selling author, speaker, serial entrepreneur, and Silicon Valley legend, tweeted, "You may find this hard to believe, but I am an introvert. I have a 'role' to play, but I fundamentally am a loner." Kawasaki's tweet set the world of social media buzzing. "At the time," wrote one blogger, "Guy's avatar featured him wearing a pink boa from a large party he threw at his house. Guy Kawasaki an introvert? Does not compute." On August 15, 2008, Pete Cashmore, the founder of Mashable, the online guide to social media, weighed in. "Wouldn't it be a great irony," he asked, "if the leading proponents of the 192/929 'it's about people' mantra weren't so enamored with meeting large groups of people in real life? Perhaps social media affords us the control we lack in real life socializing: the screen as a barrier between us and the world." Then Cashmore outed himself. "Throw me firmly in the 'introverts' camp with Guy," he posted. Studies have shown that, indeed, introverts are more likely than extroverts to express intimate facts about themselves online that their family and friends would be surprised to read, to say that they can express the "real me" online, and to spend more time in certain kinds of online discussions. They welcome the chance to communicate digitally. The same person who would never raise his hand in a lecture hall of two hundred people might blog to two thousand, or two million, without 193/929 thinking twice. The same person who finds it difficult to introduce himself to strangers might establish a presence online and then extend these relationships into the real world. What would have happened if the Subarctic Survival Situation had been conducted online, with the benefit of all the voices in the room—the Rosa Parkses and the Craig Newmarks and the Darwin Smiths? What if it had been a group of proactive castaways led by an introvert with a gift for calmly encouraging them to contribute? What if there had been an introvert and an extrovert sharing the helm, like Rosa Parks and Martin Luther King Jr.? 194/929 Might they have reached the right result? It's impossible to say. No one has ever run these studies, as far as I know—which is a shame. It's understandable that the HBS model of leadership places such a high premium on confidence and quick decision-making. If assertive people tend to get their way, then it's a useful skill for leaders whose work depends on influencing others. Decisiveness inspires confidence, while wavering (or even appearing to waver) can threaten morale. But one can take these truths too far; in some circumstances quiet, modest styles of leadership may be equally or more effective. As I left the HBS campus, I stopped by a display of notable Wall Street Journal cartoons in the Baker Library lobby. One showed a 195/929 haggard executive looking at a chart of steeply falling profits. "It's all because of Fradkin," the executive tells his colleague. "He has terrible business sense but great leadership skills, and everyone is following him down the road to ruin." Does God Love Introverts? An Evangelical's Dilemma If Harvard Business School is an East Coast enclave for the global elite, my next stop was an institution that's much the opposite. It sits on a sprawling, 120-acre campus in the former desert and current exurb of Lake Forest, California. Unlike Harvard Business School, it admits anyone who wants to join. Families stroll the palm-tree-lined plazas and walkways in good-natured 196/929 clumps. Children frolic in man-made streams and waterfalls. Staff wave amiably as they cruise by in golf carts. Wear whatever you want: sneakers and flip-flops are perfectly fine. This campus is presided over not by nattily attired professors wielding words like protagonist and case method, but by a benign Santa Claus–like figure in a Hawaiian shirt and sandy-haired goatee. With an average weekly attendance of 22,000 and counting, Saddleback Church is one of the largest and most influential evangelical churches in the nation. Its leader is Rick Warren, author of The Purpose Driven Life, one of the best-selling books of all time, and the man who delivered the invocation at President Obama's inauguration. Saddleback doesn't cater to world-famous leaders the way HBS does, but it 197/929 plays no less mighty a role in society. Evangelical leaders have the ear of presidents; dominate thousands of hours of TV time; and run multimilliondollar businesses, with the most prominent boasting their own production companies, recording studios, and distribution deals with media giants like Time Warner. Saddleback also has one more thing in common with Harvard Business School: its debt to—and propagation of—the Culture of Personality. It's a Sunday morning in August 2006, and I'm standing at the center of a dense hub of sidewalks on Saddleback's campus. I consult a signpost, the kind you see at Walt Disney World, with cheerful arrows pointing every which way: Worship Center, Plaza Room, Terrace Café, Beach Café. A nearby poster features a beaming young 198/ 929 man in bright red polo shirt and sneakers: "Looking for a new direction? Give traffic ministry a try!" I'm searching for the open-air bookstore, where

I'll be meeting Adam McHugh, a local evangelical pastor with whom I've been corresponding. McHugh is an avowed introvert, and we've been having a cross-country conversation about what it feels like to be a quiet and cerebral type in the evangelical movement—especially as a leader. Like HBS, evangelical churches often make extroversion a prerequisite for leadership, sometimes explicitly. "The priest must be … an extrovert who enthusiastically engages members and newcomers, a team player," reads an ad for a position as associate rector of a 1,400-member parish. A senior priest at another church confesses online that he has advised parishes recruiting a new 199/929 rector to ask what his or her MyersBriggs score is. "If the first letter isn't an 'E' [for extrovert]," he tells them, "think twice … I'm sure our Lord was [an extrovert]." McHugh doesn't fit this description. He discovered his introversion as a junior at Claremont McKenna College, when he realized he was getting up early in the morning just to savor time alone with a steaming cup of coffee. He enjoyed parties, but found himself leaving early. "Other people would get louder and louder, and I would get quieter and quieter," he told me. He took a Myers-Briggs personality test and found out that there was a word, introvert, that described the type of person who likes to spend time as he did. At first McHugh felt good about carving out more time for himself. But then he got active in evangelicalism 200/929 and began to feel guilty about all that solitude. He even believed that God disapproved of his choices and, by extension, of him. "The evangelical culture ties together faithfulness with extroversion," McHugh explained. "The emphasis is on community, on participating in more and more programs and events, on meeting more and more people. It's a constant tension for many introverts that they're not living that out. And in a religious world, there's more at stake when you feel that tension. It doesn't feel like 'I'm not doing as well as I'd like.' It feels like 'God isn't pleased with me.' " From outside the evangelical community, this seems an astonishing confession. Since when is solitude one of the Seven Deadly Sins? But to a fellow evangelical, McHugh's sense of spiritual 201/929 failure would make perfect sense. Contemporary evangelicalism says that every person you fail to meet and proselytize is another soul you might have saved. It also emphasizes building community among confirmed believers, with many churches encouraging (or even requiring) their members to join extracurricular groups organized around every conceivable subject—cooking, real-estate investing, skateboarding. So every social event McHugh left early, every morning he spent alone, every group he failed to join, meant wasted chances to connect with others. But, ironically, if there was one thing McHugh knew, it was that he wasn't alone. He looked around and saw a vast number of people in the evangelical community who felt just as conflicted as he did. He became ordained as a 202/929 Presbyterian minister and worked with a team of student leaders at Claremont College, many of whom were introverts. The team became a kind of laboratory for experimenting with introverted forms of leadership and ministry. They focused on one-on-one and small group interactions rather than on large groups, and McHugh helped the students find rhythms in their lives that allowed them to claim the solitude they needed and enjoyed, and to have social energy left over for leading others. He urged them to find the courage to speak up and take risks in meeting new people. A few years later, when social media exploded and evangelical bloggers started posting about their experiences, written evidence of the schism between introverts and extroverts within the evangelical church finally emerged. 203/929 One blogger wrote about his "cry from the heart wondering how to fit in as an introvert in a church that prides itself on extroverted evangelism. There are probably quite a few [of you] out there who are put on guilt trips each time [you] get a personal evangelism push at church. There's a place in God's kingdom for sensitive, reflective types. It's not easy to claim, but it's there." Another wrote about his simple desire "to serve the Lord but not serve on a parish committee. In a universal church, there should be room for the un-gregarious." McHugh added his own voice to this chorus, first with a blog calling for greater emphasis on religious practices of solitude and contemplation, and later with a book called Introverts in the Church: Finding Our Place in an Extroverted Culture. He argues that evangelism 204/929 means listening as well as talking, that evangelical churches should incorporate silence and mystery into religious worship, and that they should make room for introverted leaders who might be able to demonstrate a quieter path to God. After all, hasn't prayer always been about contemplation as well as community? Religious leaders from Jesus to Buddha, as well as the lesserknown saints, monks, shamans, and prophets, have always gone off alone to experience the revelations they later shared with the rest of us. When finally I find my way to the bookstore, McHugh is waiting with a serene expression on his face. He's in his early thirties, tall and broad205/929 shouldered, dressed in jeans, a black polo shirt, and black flip-flops. With his short brown hair, reddish goatee, and sideburns, McHugh looks like a typical Gen Xer, but he speaks in the soothing, considered tones of a college professor. McHugh doesn't preach or worship at Saddleback, but we've chosen to meet here because it's such an important symbol of evangelical culture. Since services are just about to start, there's little time to chat. Saddleback offers six different "worship venues," each housed in its own building or tent and set to its own beat: Worship Center, Traditional, OverDrive Rock, Gospel, Family, and something called Ohana Island Style Worship. We head to the main Worship Center, where Pastor Warren is about to preach. With its sky-high ceiling crisscrossed with klieg lights, the auditorium looks like a 206/929 rock concert venue, save for the unobtrusive wooden cross hanging on the side of the room. A man named Skip is warming up the congregation with a song. The lyrics are broadcast on five Jumbotron screens, interspersed with photos of shimmering lakes and Caribbean sunsets. Miked-up tech guys sit on a thronelike dais at the center of the room, training their video cameras on the audience. The cameras linger on a teenage girl—long, silky blond hair, electric smile, and shining blue eyes—who's singing her heart out. I can't help but think of Tony Robbins's "Unleash the Power Within" seminar. Did Tony base his program on megachurches like Saddleback, I wonder, or is it the other way around? "Good morning, everybody!" beams Skip, then urges us to greet those 207/929 seated near us. Most people oblige with wide smiles and glad hands, including McHugh, but there's a hint of strain beneath his smile. Pastor Warren takes the stage. He's wearing a short-sleeved polo shirt and his famous goatee. Today's sermon will be based on the book of Jeremiah, he tells us. "It would be foolish to start a business without a business plan," Warren says, "but most people have no life plan. If you're a business leader, you need to read the book of Jeremiah over and over, because he was a genius CEO." There are no Bibles at our seats, only pencils and note cards, with the key points from the sermon preprinted, and blanks to fill in as Warren goes along. Like Tony Robbins, Pastor Warren seems truly well-meaning; he's created this vast Saddleback ecosystem out of 208/ 929 nothing, and he's done good works around the world. But at the same time I can see how hard it must be, inside this world of Luau worship and Jumbotron prayer, for Saddleback's introverts to feel good about themselves. As the service wears on, I feel the same sense of alienation that McHugh has described. Events like this don't give me the sense of oneness others seem to enjoy; it's always been private occasions that make me feel connected to the joys and sorrows of the world, often in the form of communion with writers and musicians I'll never meet in person. Proust called these moments of unity between writer and reader "that fruitful miracle of a communication in the midst of solitude." His use of religious language was surely no accident. McHugh, as if reading my mind, turns to me when the service is over. 209/929 "Everything in the service involved communication," he says with gentle exasperation. "Greeting people, the lengthy sermon, the singing. There was no emphasis on quiet, liturgy, ritual, things that give you space for contemplation." McHugh's discomfort is all the more poignant because he genuinely admires Saddleback and all that it stands for. "Saddleback is doing amazing things around the world and in its own community," he says. "It's a friendly, hospitable place that genuinely seeks to connect with newcomers. That's an impressive mission given how colossal the church is, and how easy it would be for people to remain completely disconnected from others. Greeters, the informal atmosphere, meeting people around you—these are all motivated by good desires." 210/ 929 Yet McHugh finds practices like the mandatory smile-and-good-morning at the start of the service to be painful—and though he personally is willing to endure it, even sees the value in it, he worries about how many other introverts will not. "It sets up an extroverted atmosphere that can be difficult for introverts like me," he explains. "Sometimes I feel like I'm going through the motions. The outward enthusiasm and passion that seems to be part and parcel of Saddleback's culture doesn't feel natural. Not that introverts can't be eager and enthusiastic, but we're not as overtly expressive as extroverts. At a place like Saddleback, you can start questioning your own experience of God. Is it really as strong as that of other people who look the part of the devout believer?" 211/929 Evangelicalism has taken the Extrovert Ideal to its logical extreme, McHugh is telling us. If you don't love Jesus out loud, then it must not be real love. It's not enough to forge your own spiritual connection to the divine; it must be displayed publicly. Is it any wonder that introverts like Pastor McHugh start to question their own hearts? It's brave of McHugh, whose spiritual and professional calling depends on his connection to God, to confess his selfdoubt. He does so because he wants to spare others the inner conflict he has struggled with, and because he loves evangelicalism and wants it to grow by learning from the introverts in its midst. But he knows that meaningful change will come slowly to a religious culture that sees extroversion not only as a personality trait but also as an indicator of 212/929 virtue. Righteous behavior is not so much the good we do behind closed doors when no one is there to praise us; it is what we "put out into the world." Just as Tony Robbins's aggressive upselling is OK with his fans because spreading helpful ideas is part of being a good person, and just as HBS expects its students to be talkers because this is seen as a prerequisite of leadership, so have many evangelicals come to associate godliness with sociability.

CHAPTER THREE

WHEN COLLABORATION KILLS CREATIVITY

I am a horse for a single harness, not cut out for tandem or teamwork ... for well I know that in order to attain any definite goal, it is imperative that one person do the thinking and the commanding. —ALBERT EINSTEIN March 5, 1975. A cold and drizzly evening in Menlo Park, California. Thirty unprepossessing-looking engineers gather in the garage of an unemployed colleague named Gordon French. They call themselves the Homebrew Computer Club, and this is their first meeting. Their mission: to make computers accessible to regular people—no small task at a time when most computers are temperamental SUV-sized machines that only universities and corporations can afford. The garage is drafty, but the engineers leave the doors open to the damp night air so people can wander inside. In walks an uncertain young man of twenty-four, a calculator designer for Hewlett-Packard. Serious and bespectacled, he has shoulder-length hair and a brown beard. He takes a chair and listens quietly as the others marvel over a new build-it-yourself computer called the Altair 8800, which recently made the cover of Popular Electronics. The Altair isn't a true personal computer; it's hard to use, and appeals only to the 215/929 type of person who shows up at a garage on a rainy Wednesday night to talk about microchips. But it's an important first step. The young man, whose name is Stephen Wozniak, is thrilled to hear of the Altair. He's been obsessed with electronics since the age of three. When he was eleven he came across a magazine article about the first computer, the ENIAC, or Electronic Numerical Integrator and Computer, and ever since, his dream has been to build a machine so small and easy to use that you could keep it at home. And now, inside this garage, here is news that The Dream—he thinks of it with capital letters—might one day materialize. As he'll later recall in his memoir, iWoz, where most of this story appears, Wozniak is also excited to be surrounded by kindred spirits. To the 216/929 Homebrew crowd, computers are a tool for social justice, and he feels the same way. Not that he talks to anyone at this first meeting—he's way too shy for that. But that night he goes home and sketches his first design for a personal computer, with a keyboard and a screen just like the kind we use today. Three months later he builds a prototype of that machine. And ten months after that, he and Steve Jobs cofound Apple Computer. Today Steve Wozniak is a revered figure in Silicon Valley—there's a street in San Jose, California, named Woz's Way—and is sometimes called the nerd soul of Apple. He has learned over time to open up and speak publicly, even appearing as a contestant on Dancing with the Stars, where he displayed an endearing mixture of stiffness and good cheer. I once saw Wozniak speak at a 217/929 bookstore in New York City. A standing-room-only crowd showed up bearing their 1970s Apple operating manuals, in honor of all that he had done for them. But the credit is not Wozniak's alone; it also belongs to Homebrew. Wozniak identifies that first meeting as the beginning of the computer revolution and one of the most important nights of his life. So if you wanted to replicate the conditions that made Woz so productive, you might point to Homebrew, with its collection of like-minded souls. You might decide that Wozniak's achievement was a shining example of the collaborative approach to creativity. You might conclude that people 218/929 who hope to be innovative should work in highly social workplaces. And you might be wrong. Consider what Wozniak did right after the meeting in Menlo Park. Did he huddle with fellow club members to work on computer design? No. (Although he did keep attending the meetings, every other Wednesday.) Did he seek out a big, open office space full of cheerful pandemonium in which ideas would cross-pollinate? No. When you read his account of his work process on that first PC, the most striking thing is that he was always by himself. Wozniak did most of the work inside his cubicle at Hewlett-Packard. He'd arrive around 6:30 a.m. and, alone in the early morning, read engineering magazines, study chip manuals, and prepare designs in his head. After work, he'd go home, make a quick spaghetti 219/929 or TV dinner, then drive back to the office and work late into the night. He describes this period of quiet midnights and solitary sunrises as "the biggest high ever." His efforts paid off on the night of June 29, 1975, at around 10:00 p.m., when Woz finished building a prototype of his machine. He hit a few keys on the keyboard—and letters appeared on the screen in front of him. It was the sort of breakthrough moment that most of us can only dream of. And he was alone when it happened. Intentionally so. In his memoir, he offers this advice to kids who aspire to great creativity: Most inventors and engineers I've met are like me—they're shy and they live in their heads. They're almost like artists. In fact, the very best of them are artists. And artists 220/929 work best alone where they can control an invention's design without a lot of other people designing it for marketing or some other committee. I don't believe anything really revolutionary has been invented by committee. If you're that rare engineer who's an inventor and also an artist, I'm going to give you some advice that might be hard to take. That advice is: Work alone. You're going to be best able to design revolutionary products and features if you're working on your own. Not on a committee. Not on a team. From 1956 to 1962, an era best remembered for its ethos of stultifying conformity, the Institute of Personality 221/929 Assessment and Research at the University of California, Berkeley, conducted a series of studies on the nature of creativity. The researchers sought to identify the most spectacularly creative people and then figure out what made them different from everybody else. They assembled a list of architects, mathematicians, scientists, engineers, and writers who had made major contributions to their fields, and invited them to Berkeley for a weekend of personality tests, problem-solving experiments, and probing questions. Then the researchers did something similar with members of the same professions whose contributions were decidedly less groundbreaking. One of the most interesting findings, echoed by later studies, was that the more creative people tended to be socially poised introverts. They were 222/929 interpersonally skilled but "not of an especially sociable or participative temperament." They described themselves as independent and individualistic. As teens, many had been shy and solitary. These findings don't mean that introverts are always more creative than extroverts, but they do suggest that in a group of people who have been extremely creative throughout their lifetimes, you're likely to find a lot of introverts. Why should this be true? Do quiet personalities come with some ineffable quality that fuels creativity? Perhaps, as we'll see in chapter 6. But there's a less obvious yet surprisingly powerful explanation for introverts' creative advantage—an explanation that everyone can learn from: introverts prefer to work independently, and solitude can be a catalyst to innovation. As the influential psychologist Hans 223/929 Eysenck once observed, introversion "concentrates the mind on the tasks in hand, and prevents the dissipation of energy on social and sexual matters unrelated to work." In other words, if you're in the backyard sitting under a tree while everyone else is clinking glasses on the patio, you're more likely to have an apple fall on your head. (Newton was one of the world's great introverts. William Wordsworth described him as "A mind forever / Voyaging through strange seas of Thought alone.") If this is true—if solitude is an important key to creativity—then we might all want to develop a taste for it. We'd want to teach our kids to work 224/929 independently. We'd want to give employees plenty of privacy and autonomy. Yet increasingly we do just the opposite. We like to believe that we live in a grand age of creative individualism. We look back at the midcentury era in which the Berkeley researchers conducted their creativity studies, and feel superior. Unlike the starched-shirted conformists of the 1950s, we hang posters of Einstein on our walls, his tongue stuck out iconoclastically. We consume indie music and films, and generate our own online content. We "think different" (even if we got the idea from Apple Computer's famous ad campaign). But the way we organize many of our most important institutions—our schools and our workplaces—tells a very different story. It's the story of a 225/929 contemporary phenomenon that I call the New Groupthink—a phenomenon that has the potential to stifle productivity at work and to deprive schoolchildren of the skills they'll need to achieve excellence in an increasingly competitive world. The New Groupthink elevates teamwork above all else. It insists that creativity and intellectual achievement come from a gregarious place. It has many powerful advocates. "Innovation—the heart of the knowledge economy—is fundamentally social," writes the prominent journalist Malcolm Gladwell. "None of us is as smart as all of us," declares the organizational consultant Warren Bennis, in his book Organizing Genius, whose opening chapter heralds the rise of the "Great Group" and "The End of the Great Man." "Many jobs that we regard as the 226/929 province of a single mind actually require a crowd," muses Clay Shirky in his influential book Here Comes Everybody. Even "Michelangelo had assistants paint part of the Sistine Chapel ceiling." (Never mind that the assistants were likely interchangeable, while Michelangelo was not.) The New Groupthink is embraced by many corporations, which increasingly organize workforces into teams, a practice that gained popularity in the early 1990s. By 2000 an estimated half of all U.S. organizations used teams, and today virtually all of them do, according to the management professor Frederick Morgeson. A recent survey found that 91 percent of high-level managers believe that teams are the key to success. The consultant Stephen Harvill told me that of the thirty major organizations he worked with in 2010, 227/929 including J.C. Penney, Wells Fargo, Dell Computers, and Prudential, he couldn't think of a single one that didn't use teams. Some of these teams are virtual, working together from remote locations, but others demand a tremendous amount of face-to-face interaction, in the form of team-building exercises and retreats, shared online calendars that announce employees' availability for meetings, and physical workplaces that afford little privacy. Today's employees inhabit open office plans, in which no one has a room of his or her own, the only walls are the ones holding up the building, and senior executives operate from the center of the boundary-less floor along with everyone else. In fact, over 70 percent of today's employees work in an open plan; companies using them include Procter & Gamble, Ernst 228/929 & Young, GlaxoSmithKline, Alcoa, and H.J. Heinz. The amount of space per employee shrank from 500 square feet in the 1970s to 200 square feet in 2010, according to Peter Miscovich, a managing director at the real estate brokerage firm Jones Lang LaSalle. "There has been a shift from 'I' to 'we' work," Steelcase CEO James Hackett told Fast Company magazine in 2005. "Employees used to work alone in 'I' settings. Today, working in teams and groups is highly valued. We are designing products to facilitate that." Rival office manufacturer Herman Miller, Inc., has not only introduced new furniture designed to accommodate "the move toward collaboration and teaming in the workplace" but also moved its own top executives from private offices to an open space. In 2006, the Ross School of 229/929 Business at the University of Michigan demolished a classroom building in part because it wasn't set up for maximum group interaction. The New Groupthink is also practiced in our schools, via an increasingly popular method of instruction called "cooperative" or "small group" learning. In many elementary schools, the traditional rows of seats facing the teacher have been replaced with "pods" of four or more desks pushed together to facilitate countless group learning activities. Even subjects like math and creative writing, which would seem to depend on solo flights of thought, are often taught as group projects. In one fourthgrade classroom I visited, a big sign announced the "Rules for Group Work," including, YOU CAN'T ASK A TEACHER FOR HELP UNLESS EVERYONE IN YOUR GROUP HAS THE SAME QUESTION. 230/929 According to a 2002 nationwide survey of more than 1,200 fourth- and eighth-grade teachers, 55 percent of fourth-grade teachers prefer cooperative learning, compared to only 26 percent who favor teacher-directed formats. Only 35 percent of fourthgrade and 29 percent of eighth-grade teachers spend more than half their classroom time on traditional instruction, while 42 percent of fourth-grade and 41 percent of eighth-grade teachers spend at least a quarter of class time on group work. Among younger teachers, small-group learning is even more popular, suggesting that the trend will continue for some time to come. The cooperative approach has politically progressive roots—the theory is that students take ownership of their education when they learn from one another—but according to elementary 231/929 school teachers I interviewed at public and private schools in New York, Michigan, and Georgia, it also trains kids to express themselves in the team culture of corporate America. "This style of teaching reflects the business community," one fifth-grade teacher in a Manhattan public school told me, "where people's respect for others is based on their verbal abilities, not their originality or insight. You have to be someone who speaks well and calls attention to yourself. It's an elitism based on something other than merit." "Today the world of business works in groups, so now the kids do it in school," a third-grade teacher in Decatur, Georgia, explained. "Cooperative learning enables skills in working as teams—skills that are in dire demand in the workplace," writes the educational consultant Bruce Williams. 232/929 Williams also identifies leadership training as a primary benefit of cooperative learning. Indeed, the teachers I met seemed to pay close attention to their students' managerial skills. In one public school I visited in downtown Atlanta, a third-grade teacher pointed out a quiet student who likes to "do his own thing." "But we put him in charge of safety patrol one morning, so he got the chance to be a leader, too," she assured me. This teacher was kind and well-intentioned, but I wonder whether students like the young safety officer would be better off if we appreciated that not everyone aspires to be a leader in the conventional sense of the word—that some people wish to fit harmoniously into the group, and others to be independent of it. Often the most highly creative people are in the latter 233/929 category. As Janet Farrall and Leonie Kronborg write in Leadership Development for the Gifted and Talented: While extroverts tend to attain leadership in public domains, introverts tend to attain leadership in theoretical and aesthetic fields. Outstanding introverted leaders, such as Charles Darwin, Marie Curie, Patrick White and Arthur Boyd, who have created either new fields of thought or rearranged existing knowledge, have spent long periods of their lives in solitude. Hence leadership does not only apply in social situations, but also occurs in more solitary situations such as developing new techniques in the arts, creating new philosophies, writing profound books and making scientific breakthroughs. 234/929 The New Groupthink did not arise at one precise moment. Cooperative learning, corporate teamwork, and open office plans emerged at different times and for different reasons. But the mighty force that pulled these trends together was the rise of the World Wide Web, which lent both cool and gravitas to the idea of collaboration. On the Internet, wondrous creations were produced via shared brainpower: Linux, the open-source operating system; Wikipedia, the online encyclopedia; MoveOn.org, the grassroots political movement. These collective productions, exponentially greater than the sum of their parts, were so awe-inspiring that we came to revere the hive mind, the wisdom of crowds, the miracle of crowdsourcing. Collaboration became a sacred concept—the key multiplier for success. 235/929 But then we took things a step further than the facts called for. We came to value transparency and to knock down walls—not only online but also in person. We failed to realize that what makes sense for the asynchronous, relatively anonymous interactions of the Internet might not work as well inside the face-to-face, politically charged, acoustically noisy confines of an openplan office. Instead of distinguishing between online and in-person interaction, we used the lessons of one to inform our thinking about the other. That's why, when people talk about aspects of the New Groupthink such as open office plans, they tend to invoke the Internet. "Employees are putting their whole lives up on Facebook and Twitter and everywhere else anyway. There's no reason they should hide behind a cubicle wall," Dan Lafontaine, 236/929 CFO of the social marketing firm Mr. Youth, told NPR. Another management consultant told me something similar: "An office wall is exactly what it sounds like—a barrier. The fresher your methodologies of thinking, the less you want boundaries. The companies who use open office plans are new companies, just like the World Wide Web, which is still a teenager." The Internet's role in promoting faceto-face group work is especially ironic because the early Web was a medium that enabled bands of often introverted individualists—people much like the solitude-craving thought leaders Farrall and Kronborg describe—to come together to subvert and transcend the usual ways of problem-solving. A significant majority of the earliest computer enthusiasts were introverts, according to a study of 1,229 computer 237/929 professionals working in the U.S., the U.K., and Australia between 1982 and 1984. "It's a truism in tech that open source attracts introverts," says Dave W. Smith, a consultant and software developer in Silicon Valley, referring to the practice of producing software by opening the source code to the online public and allowing anyone to copy, improve upon, and distribute it. Many of these people were motivated by a desire to contribute to the broader good, and to see their achievements recognized by a community they valued. But the earliest open-source creators didn't share office space—often they didn't even live in the same country. Their collaborations took place largely in the ether. This is not an insignificant detail. If you had gathered the same people who created Linux, installed them in a giant conference room for a 238/929 year, and asked them to devise a new operating system, it's doubtful that anything so revolutionary would have occurred—for reasons we'll explore in the rest of this chapter. When the research psychologist Anders Ericsson was fifteen, he took up chess. He was pretty good at it, he thought, trouncing all his classmates during lunchtime matches. Until one day a boy who'd been one of the worst players in the class started to win every match. Ericsson wondered what had happened. "I really thought about this a lot," he recalls in an interview with Daniel Coyle, author of The Talent Code. "Why could that boy, whom I had beaten so easily, now beat me just as 239/929 easily? I knew he was studying, going to a chess club, but what had happened, really, underneath?" This is the question that drives Ericsson's career: How do extraordinary achievers get to be so great at what they do? Ericsson has searched for answers in fields as diverse as chess, tennis, and classical piano. In a now-famous experiment, he and his colleagues compared three groups of expert violinists at the elite Music Academy in West Berlin. The researchers asked the professors to divide the students into three groups: the "best violinists," who had the potential for careers as international soloists; the "good violinists"; and a third group training to be violin teachers rather than performers. Then they interviewed the musicians and asked them to keep detailed diaries of their time. 240/929 They found a striking difference among the groups. All three groups spent the same amount of time—over fifty hours a week—participating in music-related activities. All three had similar classroom requirements making demands on their time. But the two best groups spent most of their musicrelated time practicing in solitude: 24.3 hours a week, or 3.5 hours a day, for the best group, compared with only 9.3 hours a week, or 1.3 hours a day, for the worst group. The best violinists rated "practice alone" as the most important of all their music-related activities. Elite musicians—even those who perform in groups—describe practice sessions with their chamber group as "leisure" compared with solo practice, where the real work gets done. Ericsson and his cohorts found similar effects of solitude when they studied 241/929 other kinds of expert performers. "Serious study alone" is the strongest predictor of skill for tournament-rated chess players, for example; grandmasters typically spend a whopping five thousand hours—almost five times as many hours as intermediate-level players—studying the game by themselves during their first ten years of learning to play. College students who tend to study alone learn more over time than those who work in groups. Even elite athletes in team sports often spend unusual amounts of time in solitary practice. What's so magical about solitude? In many fields, Ericsson told me, it's only when you're alone that you can engage in Deliberate Practice, which he has identified as the key to exceptional achievement. When you practice deliberately, you identify the tasks or 242/929 knowledge that are just out of your reach, strive to upgrade your performance, monitor your progress, and revise accordingly. Practice sessions that fall short of this standard are not only less useful—they're counterproductive. They reinforce existing cognitive mechanisms instead of improving them. Deliberate Practice is best conducted alone for several reasons. It takes intense concentration, and other people can be distracting. It requires deep motivation, often self-generated. But most important, it involves working on the task that's most challenging to you personally. Only when you're alone, Ericsson told me, can you "go directly to the part that's challenging to you. If you want to improve what you're doing, you have to be the one who generates the move. Imagine a group class—you're the one generating the 243/929 move only a small percentage of the time." To see Deliberate Practice in action, we need look no further than the story of Stephen Wozniak. The Homebrew meeting was the catalyst that inspired him to build that first PC, but the knowledge base and work habits that made it possible came from another place entirely: Woz had deliberately practiced engineering ever since he was a little kid. (Ericsson says that it takes approximately ten thousand hours of Deliberate Practice to gain true expertise, so it helps to start young.) In iWoz, Wozniak describes his childhood passion for electronics, and unintentionally recounts all the elements of Deliberate Practice that Ericsson emphasizes. First, he was motivated: his father, a Lockheed engineer, had taught Woz that engineers could change 244/929 people's lives and were "among the key people in the world." Second, he built his expertise step by painstaking step. Because he entered countless science fairs, he says, I acquired a central ability that was to help me through my entire career: patience. I'm serious. Patience is usually so underrated. I mean, for all those projects, from third grade all the way to eighth grade, I just learned things gradually, figuring out how to put electronic devices together without so much as cracking a book.... I learned to not worry so much about the outcome, but to concentrate on the step I was on and to try to do it as perfectly as I could when I was doing it. 245/929 Third, Woz often worked alone. This was not necessarily by choice. Like many technically inclined kids, he took a painful tumble down the social ladder when he got to junior high school. As a boy he'd been admired for his science prowess, but now nobody seemed to care. He hated small talk, and his interests were out of step with those of his peers. A black-and-white photo from this period shows Woz, hair closely cropped, grimacing intensely, pointing proudly at his "science-fairwinning Adder/Subtractor," a boxlike contraption of wires, knobs, and gizmos. But the awkwardness of those years didn't deter him from pursuing his dream; it probably nurtured it. He would never have learned so much about computers, Woz says now, if he hadn't been too shy to leave the house. 246/929 No one would choose this sort of painful adolescence, but the fact is that the solitude of Woz's teens, and the single-minded focus on what would turn out to be a lifelong passion, is typical for highly creative people. According to the psychologist Mihaly Csikszentmihalyi, who between 1990 and 1995 studied the lives of ninetyone exceptionally creative people in the arts, sciences, business, and government, many of his subjects were on the social margins during adolescence, partly because "intense curiosity or focused interest seems odd to their peers." Teens who are too gregarious to spend time alone often fail to cultivate their talents "because practicing music or studying math requires a solitude they dread." Madeleine L'Engle, the author of the classic young adult novel A Wrinkle in Time and more than sixty 247/929 other books, says that she would never have developed into such a bold thinker had she not spent so much of her childhood alone with books and ideas. As a young boy, Charles Darwin made friends easily but preferred to spend his time taking long, solitary nature walks. (As an adult he was no different. "My dear Mr. Babbage," he wrote to the famous mathematician who had invited him to a dinner party, "I am very much obliged to you for sending me cards for your parties, but I am afraid of accepting them, for I should meet some people there, to whom I have sworn by all the saints in Heaven, I never go out.") But exceptional performance depends not only on the groundwork we lay through Deliberate Practice; it also requires the right working conditions. 248/929 And in contemporary workplaces, these are surprisingly hard to come by. One of the side benefits of being a consultant is getting intimate access to many different work environments. Tom DeMarco, a principal of the Atlantic Systems Guild team of consultants, had walked around a good number of offices in his time, and he noticed that some workspaces were a lot more densely packed than others. He wondered what effect all that social interaction had on performance. To find out, DeMarco and his colleague Timothy Lister devised a study called the Coding War Games. The purpose of the games was to identify the characteristics of the best and worst 249/929 computer programmers; more than six hundred developers from ninety-two different companies participated. Each designed, coded, and tested a program, working in his normal office space during business hours. Each participant was also assigned a partner from the same company. The partners worked separately, however, without any communication, a feature of the games that turned out to be critical. When the results came in, they revealed an enormous performance gap. The best outperformed the worst by a 10:1 ratio. The top programmers were also about 2.5 times better than the median. When DeMarco and Lister tried to figure out what accounted for this astonishing range, the factors that you'd think would matter—such as years of experience, salary, even the time spent completing the work—had little 250/929 correlation to outcome. Programmers with ten years' experience did no better than those with two years. The half who performed above the median earned less than 10 percent more than the half below—even though they were almost twice as good. The programmers who turned in "zero-defect" work took slightly less, not more, time to complete the exercise than those who made mistakes. It was a mystery with one intriguing clue: programmers from the same companies performed at more or less the same level, even though they hadn't worked together. That's because top performers overwhelmingly worked for companies that gave their workers the most privacy, personal space, control over their physical environments, and freedom from interruption. Sixty-two percent of the best performers said that 251/929 their workspace was acceptably private, compared to only 19 percent of the worst performers; 76 percent of the worst performers but only 38 percent of the top performers said that people often interrupted them needlessly. The Coding War Games are well known in tech circles, but DeMarco and Lister's findings reach beyond the world of computer programmers. A mountain of recent data on open-plan offices from many different industries corroborates the results of the games. Open-plan offices have been found to reduce productivity and impair memory. They're associated with high staff turnover. They make people sick, hostile, unmotivated, and insecure. Open-plan workers are more likely to suffer from high blood pressure and elevated stress levels and to get the flu; they argue more with their colleagues; they worry 252/929 about coworkers eavesdropping on their phone calls and spying on their computer screens. They have fewer personal and confidential conversations with colleagues. They're often subject to loud and uncontrollable noise, which raises heart rates; releases cortisol, the body's fight-or-flight "stress" hormone; and makes people socially distant, quick to anger, aggressive, and slow to help others. Indeed, excessive stimulation seems to impede learning: a recent study found that people learn better after a quiet stroll through the woods than after a noisy walk down a city street. Another study, of 38,000 knowledge workers across different sectors, found that the simple act of being interrupted is one of the biggest barriers to productivity. Even multitasking, that prized feat of modern-day office 253/929 warriors, turns out to be a myth. Scientists now know that the brain is incapable of paying attention to two things at the same time. What looks like multitasking is really switching back and forth between multiple tasks, which reduces productivity and increases mistakes by up to 50 percent. Many introverts seem to know these things instinctively, and resist being herded together. Backbone Entertainment, a video game design company in Oakland, California, initially used an open office plan but found that their game developers, many of whom were introverts, were unhappy. "It was one big warehouse space, with just tables, no walls, and everyone could see each other," recalls Mike Mika, the former creative director. "We switched over to cubicles and were worried about it—you'd think in a creative 254/ 929 environment that people would hate that. But it turns out they prefer having nooks and crannies they can hide away in and just be away from everybody." Something similar happened at Reebok International when, in 2000, the company consolidated 1,250 employees in their new headquarters in Canton, Massachusetts. The managers assumed that their shoe designers would want office space with plenty of access to each other so they could brainstorm (an idea they probably picked up when they were getting their MBAs). Luckily, they consulted first with the shoe designers themselves, who told them that actually what they needed was peace and quiet so they could concentrate. This would not have come as news to Jason Fried, cofounder of the web application company 37signals. For ten years, beginning in 2000, Fried asked 255/929 hundreds of people (mostly designers, programmers, and writers) where they liked to work when they needed to get something done. He found that they went anywhere but their offices, which were too noisy and full of interruptions. That's why, of Fried's sixteen employees, only eight live in Chicago, where 37signals is based, and even they are not required to show up for work, even for meetings. Especially not for meetings, which Fried views as "toxic." Fried is not anti-collaboration—37signals' home page touts its products' ability to make collaboration productive and pleasant. But he prefers passive forms of collaboration like e-mail, instant messaging, and online chat tools. His advice for other employers? "Cancel your next meeting," he advises. "Don't reschedule it. Erase it from memory." He also suggests "No-Talk 256/929 Thursdays," one day a week in which employees aren't allowed to speak to each other. The people Fried interviewed were saying out loud what creative people have always known. Kafka, for example, couldn't bear to be near even his adoring fiancée while he worked: You once said that you would like to sit beside me while I write. Listen, in that case I could not write at all. For writing means revealing oneself to excess; that utmost of self-revelation and surrender, in which a human being, when involved with others, would feel he was losing himself, and from which, therefore, he will always shrink as long as he is in his right mind.... That is why one can never be alone enough when one writes, why there can never be 257/929 enough silence around one when one writes, why even night is not night enough. Even the considerably more cheerful Theodor Geisel (otherwise known as Dr. Seuss) spent his workdays ensconced in his private studio, the walls lined with sketches and drawings, in a bell-tower outside his La Jolla, California, house. Geisel was a much more quiet man than his jocular rhymes suggest. He rarely ventured out in public to meet his young readership, fretting that kids would expect a merry, outspoken, Cat in the Hat–like figure, and would be disappointed with his reserved personality. "In mass, [children] terrify me," he admitted. 258/929 If personal space is vital to creativity, so is freedom from "peer pressure." Consider the story of the legendary advertising man Alex Osborn. Today Osborn's name rings few bells, but during the first half of the twentieth century he was the kind of larger-than-life renaissance man who mesmerized his contemporaries.

Osborn was a founding partner of the advertising agency Batten, Barton, Durstine, and Osborn (BBDO), but it was as an author that he really made his mark, beginning with the day in 1938 that a magazine editor invited him to lunch and asked what his hobby was. "Imagination," replied Osborn. "Mr. Osborn," said the editor, "you must do a book on that. It's a job that has been waiting to be done all these years. There is no subject of greater 259/929 importance. You must give it the time and energy and thoroughness it deserves." And so Mr. Osborn did. He wrote several books during the 1940s and 1950s, in fact, each tackling a problem that had vexed him in his capacity as head of BBDO: his employees were not creative enough. They had good ideas, Osborn believed, but were loath to share them for fear of their colleagues' judgment. For Osborn, the solution was not to have his employees work alone, but rather to remove the threat of criticism from group work. He invented the concept of brainstorming, a process in which group members generate ideas in a nonjudgmental atmosphere. Brainstorming had four rules: 260/929 1. Don't judge or criticize ideas. 2. Be freewheeling. The wilder the idea, the better. 3. Go for quantity. The more ideas you have, the better. 4. Build on the ideas of fellow group members. Osborn believed passionately that groups—once freed from the shackles of social judgment—produced more and better ideas than did individuals working in solitude, and he made grand claims for his favored method. "The quantitative results of group brainstorming are beyond question," he wrote. "One group produced 45 suggestions for a home-appliance promotion, 56 ideas for a money-raising campaign, 124 ideas on how to sell more blankets. In another case, 15 groups 261/929 brainstormed one and the same problem and produced over 800 ideas." Osborn's theory had great impact, and company leaders took up brainstorming with enthusiasm. To this day, it's common for anyone who spends time in corporate America to find himself occasionally cooped up with colleagues in a room full of whiteboards, markers, and a preternaturally peppy facilitator encouraging everyone to free-associate. There's only one problem with Osborn's breakthrough idea: group brainstorming doesn't actually work. One of the first studies to demonstrate this was conducted in 1963. Marvin Dunnette, a psychology professor at the University of Minnesota, gathered forty-eight research scientists and forty-eight advertising executives, all of them male employees of Minnesota Mining and 262/929 Manufacturing (otherwise known as 3M, inventors of the Post-it), and asked them to participate in both solitary and group brainstorming sessions. Dunnette was confident that the executives would benefit from the group process. He was less sure that the research scientists, whom he considered more introverted, would profit from group work. Dunnette divided each set of fortyeight men into twelve groups of four. Each foursome was given a problem to brainstorm, such as the benefits or difficulties that would arise from being born with an extra thumb. Each man was also given a similar problem to brainstorm on his own. Then Dunnette and his team counted all the ideas, comparing those produced by the groups with those generated by people working individually. In order to 263/929 compare apples with apples, Dunnette pooled the ideas of each individual together with those of three other individuals, as if they had been working in "nominal" groups of four. The researchers also measured the quality of the ideas, rating them on a "Probability Scale" of 0 through 4. The results were unambiguous. The men in twenty-three of the twenty-four groups produced more ideas when they worked on their own than when they worked as a group. They also produced ideas of equal or higher quality when working individually. And the advertising executives were no better at group work than the presumably introverted research scientists. Since then, some forty years of research has reached the same startling conclusion. Studies have shown that performance gets worse as group size 264/929 increases: groups of nine generate fewer and poorer ideas compared to groups of six, which do worse than groups of four. The "evidence from science suggests that business people must be insane to use brainstorming groups," writes the organizational psychologist Adrian Furnham. "If you have talented and motivated people, they should be encouraged to work alone when creativity or efficiency is the highest priority." The one exception to this is online brainstorming. Groups brainstorming electronically, when properly managed, not only do better than individuals, research shows; the larger the group, the better it performs. The same is true of academic research—professors who work together electronically, from different physical locations, tend to produce research that is more influential 265/ 929 than those either working alone or collaborating face-to-face. This shouldn't surprise us; as we've said, it was the curious power of electronic collaboration that contributed to the New Groupthink in the first place. What created Linux, or Wikipedia, if not a gigantic electronic brainstorming session? But we're so impressed by the power of online collaboration that we've come to overvalue all group work at the expense of solo thought. We fail to realize that participating in an online working group is a form of solitude all its own. Instead we assume that the success of online collaborations will be replicated in the face-to-face world. Indeed, after all these years of evidence that conventional brainstorming groups don't work, they remain as popular as ever. Participants in brainstorming sessions usually believe that their 266/929 group performed much better than it actually did, which points to a valuable reason for their continued popularity—group brainstorming makes people feel attached. A worthy goal, so long as we understand that social glue, as opposed to creativity, is the principal benefit. Psychologists usually offer three explanations for the failure of group brainstorming. The first is social loafing: in a group, some individuals tend to sit back and let others do the work. The second is production blocking: only one person can talk or produce an idea at once, while the other group members are forced to sit passively. And the third is evaluation apprehension, 267/929 meaning the fear of looking stupid in front of one's peers. Osborn's "rules" of brainstorming were meant to neutralize this anxiety, but studies show that the fear of public humiliation is a potent force. During the 1988–89 basketball season, for example, two NCAA basketball teams played eleven games without any spectators, owing to a measles outbreak that led their schools to quarantine all students. Both teams played much better (higher free-throw percentages, for example) without any fans, even adoring home-team fans, to unnerve them. The behavioral economist Dan Ariely noticed a similar phenomenon when he conducted a study asking thirty-nine participants to solve anagram puzzles, either alone at their desks or with others watching. Ariely predicted that the 268/929 participants would do better in public because they'd be more motivated. But they performed worse. An audience may be rousing, but it's also stressful. The problem with evaluation apprehension is that there's not much we can do about it. You'd think you could overcome it with will or training or a set of group process rules like Alex Osborn's. But recent research in neuroscience suggests that the fear of judgment runs much deeper and has more far-reaching implications than we ever imagined. Between 1951 and 1956, just as Osborn was promoting the power of group brainstorming, a psychologist named Solomon Asch conducted a series of now-famous experiments on the dangers of group influence. Asch gathered student volunteers into groups and had them take a vision test. He 269/929 showed them a picture of three lines of varying lengths and asked questions about how the lines compared with one another: which was longer, which one matched the length of a fourth line, and so on. His questions were so simple that 95 percent of students answered every question correctly. But when Asch planted actors in the groups, and the actors confidently volunteered the same incorrect answer, the number of students who gave all correct answers plunged to 25 percent. That is, a staggering 75 percent of the participants went along with the group's wrong answer to at least one question. The Asch experiments demonstrated the power of conformity at exactly the time that Osborn was trying to release us from its chains. What they didn't tell us was why we were so prone to 270/929 conform. What was going on in the minds of the kowtowers? Had their perception of the lines' lengths been altered by peer pressure, or did they knowingly give wrong answers for fear of being the odd one out? For decades, psychologists puzzled over this question. Today, with the help of brain-scanning technology, we may be getting closer to the answer. In 2005 an Emory University neuroscientist named Gregory Berns decided to conduct an updated version of Asch's experiments. Berns and his team recruited thirty-two volunteers, men and women between the ages of nineteen and forty-one. The volunteers played a game in which each group member was shown two different three-dimensional objects on a computer screen and asked to decide whether the first object could be rotated to match the second. The 271/929 experimenters used an fMRI scanner to take snapshots of the volunteers' brains as they conformed to or broke with group opinion. The results were both disturbing and illuminating. First, they corroborated Asch's findings. When the volunteers played the game on their own, they gave the wrong answer only 13.8 percent of the time. But when they played with a group whose members gave unanimously wrong answers, they agreed with the group 41 percent of the time. But Berns's study also shed light on exactly why we're such conformists. When the volunteers played alone, the brain scans showed activity in a network of brain regions including the occipital cortex and parietal cortex, which are associated with visual and spatial perception, and in the frontal cortex, which is associated with conscious 272/929 decision-making. But when they went along with their group's wrong answer, their brain activity revealed something very different. Remember, what Asch wanted to know was whether people conformed despite knowing that the group was wrong, or whether their perceptions had been altered by the group. If the former was true, Berns and his team reasoned, then they should see more brain activity in the decision-making prefrontal cortex. That is, the brain scans would pick up the volunteers deciding consciously to abandon their own beliefs to fit in with the group. But if the brain scans showed heightened activity in regions associated with visual and spatial perception, this would suggest that the group had somehow managed to change the individual's perceptions. 273/ 929 That was exactly what happened—the conformists showed less brain activity in the frontal, decisionmaking regions and more in the areas of the brain associated with perception. Peer pressure, in other words, is not only unpleasant, but can actually change your view of a problem. These early findings suggest that groups are like mind-altering substances. If the group thinks the answer is A, you're much more likely to believe that A is correct, too. It's not that you're saying consciously, "Hmm, I'm not sure, but they all think the answer's A, so I'll go with that." Nor are you saying, "I want them to like me, so I'll just pretend that the answer's A." No, you are doing something much more unexpected—and dangerous. Most of Berns's volunteers reported having gone along with the group because "they thought 274/929 that they had arrived serendipitously at the same correct answer." They were utterly blind, in other words, to how much their peers had influenced them. What does this have to do with social fear? Well, remember that the volunteers in the Asch and Berns studies didn't always conform. Sometimes they picked the right answer despite their peers' influence. And Berns and his team found something very interesting about these moments. They were linked to heightened activation in the amygdala, a small organ in the brain associated with upsetting emotions such as the fear of rejection. Berns refers to this as "the pain of independence," and it has serious implications. Many of our most important civic institutions, from elections to jury trials to the very idea of majority rule, depend on dissenting voices. But when 275/929 the group is literally capable of changing our perceptions, and when to stand alone is to activate primitive, powerful, and unconscious feelings of rejection, then the health of these institutions seems far more vulnerable than we think. But of course I've been simplifying the case against face-to-face collaboration. Steve Wozniak collaborated with Steve Jobs, after all; without their pairing, there would be no Apple today. Every pair bond between mother and father, between parent and child, is an act of creative collaboration. Indeed, studies show that face-to-face interactions create trust in a way that online interactions can't. Research also suggests that 276/929 population density is correlated with innovation; despite the advantages of quiet walks in the woods, people in crowded cities benefit from the web of interactions that urban life offers. I have experienced this phenomenon personally. When

I was getting ready to write this book, I carefully set up my home office, complete with uncluttered desk, file cabinets, free counter space, and plenty of natural light—and then felt too cut off from the world to type a single keystroke there. Instead, I wrote most of this book on a laptop at my favorite densely packed neighborhood café. I did this for exactly the reasons that champions of the New Groupthink might suggest: the mere presence of other people helped my mind to make associative leaps. The coffee shop was full of people bent over their own computers, and if the expressions of rapt 277/929 concentration on their faces were any indication, I wasn't the only one getting a lot of work done. But the café worked as my office because it had specific attributes that are absent from many modern schools and workplaces. It was social, yet its casual, come-and-go-as-you-please nature left me free from unwelcome entanglements and able to "deliberately practice" my writing. I could toggle back and forth between observer and social actor as much as I wanted. I could also control my environment. Each day I chose the location of my table—in the center of the room or along the perimeter—depending on whether I wanted to be seen as well as to see. And I had the option to leave whenever I wanted peace and quiet to edit what I'd written that day. Usually I was ready to exercise this right after only a few 278/929 hours—not the eight, ten, or fourteen hours that many office dwellers put in. The way forward, I'm suggesting, is not to stop collaborating face-to-face, but to refine the way we do it. For one thing, we should actively seek out symbiotic introvert-extrovert relationships, in which leadership and other tasks are divided according to people's natural strengths and temperaments. The most effective teams are composed of a healthy mix of introverts and extroverts, studies show, and so are many leadership structures. We also need to create settings in which people are free to circulate in a shifting kaleidoscope of interactions, and to disappear into their private workspaces when they want to focus or simply be alone. Our schools should teach children the skills to work with others—cooperative learning can be 279/929 effective when practiced well and in moderation—but also the time and training they need to deliberately practice on their own. It's also vital to recognize that many people—especially introverts like Steve Wozniak—need extra quiet and privacy in order to do their best work. Some companies are starting to understand the value of silence and solitude, and are creating "flexible" open plans that offer a mix of solo workspaces, quiet zones, casual meeting areas, cafés, reading rooms, computer hubs, and even "streets" where people can chat casually with each other without interrupting others' workflow. At Pixar Animation Studios, the sixteen-acre campus is built around a football-field-sized atrium housing mailboxes, a cafeteria, and even bathrooms. The idea is to encourage as 280/929 many casual, chance encounters as possible. At the same time, employees are encouraged to make their individual offices, cubicles, desks, and work areas their own and to decorate them as they wish. Similarly, at Microsoft, many employees enjoy their own private offices, yet they come with sliding doors, movable walls, and other features that allow occupants to decide when they want to collaborate and when they need private time to think. These kinds of diverse workspaces benefit introverts as well as extroverts, the systems design researcher Matt Davis told me, because they offer more spaces to retreat to than traditional open-plan offices. I suspect that Wozniak himself would approve of these developments. Before he created the Apple PC, Woz designed calculators at Hewlett-Packard, a job he 281/929 loved in part because HP made it so easy to chat with others. Every day at 10:00 a.m. and 2:00 p.m. management wheeled in donuts and coffee, and people would socialize and swap ideas. What set these interactions apart was how low-key and relaxed they were. In iWoz, he recalls HP as a meritocracy where it didn't matter what you looked like, where there was no premium on playing social games, and where no one pushed him from his beloved engineering work into management. That was what collaboration meant for Woz: the ability to share a donut and a brainwave with his laid-back, nonjudgmental, poorly dressed colleagues—who minded not a whit when he disappeared into his cubicle to get the real work done.

www.ingramcontent.com/pod-product-compliance
Lightning Source LLC
Chambersburg PA
CBHW052219150726
48002CB00003B/1186